Fairview's Guide to Composition and Essay Writing

Fairview's Guide to Composition and Essay Writing

Gabriel Arquilevich, M.F.A.

Fairview Publishing
Ventura County, California

Requests for permission and for orders should be mailed to the following address: Fairview Publishing, P.O. Box 746, Oak View, CA 93022.

Printed in the United States of America

ISBN: 0-9649042-1-7

ACKNOWLEDGMENTS

Many thanks to Ron Arquilevich for his help with layout and for designing the cover of the book. Thanks to John Duncan for his editing help, and to David Howard for his ongoing support. Thank you to Mark Garcia, James Usher, Nao Braverman, and Dan Helfman for their essay contributions. To Jaymie, Millie, Isaac, and Holden, thank you for your love and support.

ABOUT THE AUTHOR

Gabriel Arquilevich holds a B.A. in English from Johnston College at the University of Redlands and an M.F.A. in Poetry from the University of Massachusetts in Amherst. In addition to his nine years of teaching experience, he is the author of numerous educational publications, including *Writing for 100 Days* (Fairview), *World Religions* (Teacher Created Materials), and the complete high school literature curricula for Oak Meadow School, a home schooling center based in Putney, VT. Currently, in addition to his work as a freelance writer, Mr. Arquilevich teaches English at Ventura Community College, in Ventura, CA. He lives in Ojai with his wife and three children.

Introduction to Teachers

Fairview's Guide to Composition and Essay Writing fulfills the need for a friendly but demanding high school level composition book. That this need persists in the first place is unfortunate. In too many cases, we teach students the five paragraph essay, assign a few book reports and research papers, and ultimately we are either unwilling or unable to move students further along in the composition process. Not only does this stunt the students' writing and critical thinking abilities, but it also limits their appreciation of these processes, and they may fail to see the depth and creativity involved in composition and essay writing.

We could attribute this dead end to a lack of skills on their part, or to a culture that reads and writes less all the time. While these causes may be valid, it is helpful to understand how we contribute to this shortcoming and how we can help students elevate both their writing skills and their appreciation for the craft. As you will see, it is not that we ask too much of our students—we ask too little.

First, we should look to our own impressions of composition and essay writing. Many of us who practiced sentence diagramming and abided by strict paragraphing rules found the process to be pure drudgery. "I like to write stories, but I hate writing essays," is a litany heard from students everywhere. Subconsciously, many of us agree.

Returning again to the source, we discover that unless we love writing to begin with, we are rarely introduced to the creativeness involved in writing essays. While sentence diagramming and formal structures are helpful, we are not moved beyond these aids; we are not inspired. Our essays become statements of facts pinned together by predictable transitions, and then framed by a thesis statement introduction and an "In conclusion" final paragraph. As long as our mechanics are sound, we receive a good grade and move on. It's no wonder that essays are among the most maligned form of writing.

In response to this mindset, a recurring theme is echoed throughout this book: *Essay writing and composition are creative acts.* This may be a discovery we have yet to make for ourselves, and one that we must learn to foster in our students. For example, a student writes a persuasive paper about the exercises of commercial fishing: "Trawlers drag extremely large nets, which scoop up everything they pass over." Fine. But it can be better, more visceral, more creative: "Trawlers drag gigantic nets, which indiscriminately scoop up bass, halibut, and unsuspecting dolphin." Is this a creative act of revision? Of course it is. The illustrative details give the sentence more impact and more appeal.

Naturally, there are limits and specific challenges to the essay form. Essays are not fiction, though the boundary can be vague; and while essays are not poetry, they can be very poetic. Some essays require direct quotes for support. Furthermore, it takes time and hard work to achieve sentence variety and fluidity. While revising, students must learn to look at every sentence they write with a critical eye. All this is difficult, but *if students awaken to the possibilities involved, they will be inspired to sharpen their craft.* After all, the essay is a form of expression, and we all like to express ourselves. It is the goal of *Fairview's Guide* to introduce some of these possibilities.

Note: Like its predecessor, *Writing for 100 Days*, this book begins with the assumption that students have a relatively firm grasp on rudimentary punctuation and grammar. While there is instruction regarding the rules and strategies of quote incorporation, *Fairview's Guide* focuses primarily on elements of composition. Those of you familiar with *100 Days* will find limited overlap. Moreover, the shared elements are examined here in a more sophisticated manner.

THE SECTIONS OF THE BOOK

It is vital that you review the structure of *Fairview's Guide* carefully before beginning. The four sections are distinct in their offerings.

- **The Big Picture**: Beginning with an emphasis on illustrative writing, the section continues with a study of tone, audience, and paragraphing. After a look at introductions and conclusions, the section guides students from brainstorming to drafting.

- **Sentence Fluidity**: The next section is devoted to helping students achieve fluid writing by teaching them to identify and correct awkward sentences, and to achieve precision in word choice, transitioning and quote incorporation. An answer key for all exercises is located at the end of the book.

- **Sentence Combining**: This section provides sentence combining exercises to assist students in learning to economize their writing while employing a variety of sentence structures. These "grind it out" assignments will result in more sophisticated and creative prose.

- **Four Essays**: What students have learned is put into application as they are introduced to four types of essays. The essays are chosen for their variety, each demanding a different quality of reasoning, spirit and structure. Each part features a sample student piece meant for study and inspiration. In addition, students are encouraged to peer edit one another's work. Let's take a closer look:

    (1) ***Taking a Stand***— By taking an assertive stand on an issue, students discover the importance of a balanced, well supported argument.

    (2) ***Compare and Contrast***— By highlighting the similarities and differences of a topic, students learn to create meaning.

(3)***Personal Essay***— By focusing on an event, a relationship or a place, students learn to structure memories and observances for the purpose of discovery.

(4) ***Mock Essay***—This assignment challenges students to either imitate an essay form or to imitate an author's style. While the mock essay is fun, it is also demanding because students must study and apply a form or style foreign to their own.

A note on grading: Please be aware that there are alternatives to standard letter grades. You may consider having a point total, establishing a value for different features. Mechanics might be 25 points, structure 25, and so forth. If you use letter grades, try giving two grades: one for content and one for writing. Most importantly, be sure that grading does not interfere with genuine feedback and evaluation. The more care you put into a student's work, the more likely she is to understand and respond to your comments.

THE READING CONNECTION & THE READING JOURNAL

This is a valuable complement to the writing practice, for here we can learn about writing by studying other writers. As students read and respond to more essays, they will begin to recognize strategies, see different writing styles, and awaken to new possibilities. Therefore, it is recommended that students begin on an essay reading binge!

As you will see from the instruction on page 2, students are encouraged to read a variety of authors and essay styles. Are there contemporary or regional essayists that the student would find interesting? If the student has a hobby, look for essays that relate.

Throughout, students are asked to look for examples of what they're studying. After reading about the importance of introductions and conclusions, for instance, students read the openings and closings of several essays. They will write about the authors' strategies in their journals.

HOW TO USE *FAIRVIEW'S GUIDE*

As suggested earlier, it is important that you and your students acquaint yourselves with *Fairview's Guide* before beginning. While the text builds on some principles, it is malleable. It is recommended, however, that students begin with the section on illustrative writing (page 3), since so much of the material echoes back to this foundation. From this point **consider beginning with an essay writing assignment while tending to the skill development as you go**. If the composition exercises get tedious, space them out. If a student already writes with a great deal of variety she might not benefit from the sentence combining section.

There is no time frame for completing this book. It can be used as a supplement to a literature component, or it can be used exclusively for a period of time. Use your best judgment. Just be sure not to move a student along too quickly. It is far more important that he write one good essay than it is for him to complete the whole book in a set amount of time. For if he can write one good essay, he can write another.

TEACHING TIPS

- Before beginning, encourage students to express their feelings about writing and about essays in particular. This will be an opportunity for a heartfelt discussion while ensuring a clean starting point.

- Look for opportunities to highlight the relevance of writing. Can you get a published writer to speak to a group of students? How about a bulletin board featuring contemporary essays alongside student work?

- Use overhead transparencies to study essays. This allows the class to look at a piece together, whether it be a published model or a student's work.

- Discuss published essays with students. Help them pinpoint writing techniques and allow them to share their insights.

- Encourage students to personalize the cover of their reading journals, and to add creative thoughts and illustrations throughout.

- In addition to peer editing, ask students to present their essays to their peers. The student could read the whole piece aloud, deliver it as a speech, or simply touch on the major points. Encourage students to use visual aids to complement their presentations.

- If there is an opportunity for improvement, challenge students to rewrite their essays. Help them to see the value of looking at every sentence they write. In assigning a rewrite, be careful not to assume a punitive tone. You should be able to sense when it is time to move on to another assignment.

- Awaken students to the fact that essays can be funny, spirited, and emotional.

A WORD FOR HOME SCHOOLERS

Like *Writing for 100 Days, Fairview's Guide* lends itself nicely to home schooling. The self-directed student will find ample opportunity to learn on her own. Those lessons that call for interaction can be fulfilled with a parent or a home schooling group.

One recommendation: Once the student completes each of his essays, allow for more than one peer editing response. This will ensure that he receives a variety of feedback, which is always healthy when it comes to writing.

Table of Contents

The Big Picture

The Reading Journal

The reading journal is an important complement to *Fairview's Guide*. Let's take a moment to explain what it is and why it's beneficial.

Most of us read solely for content. When discussing an essay, we say "what it's about." As students of writing we must take the next step and ask ourselves questions about how an essay is written. This will open our eyes to the great number of choices a writer must make—from paragraphing to word choice to structure. We want to have a relationship to the material, not to merely consume it.

The kind of attention to detail we're seeking doesn't come easily. It's a learned skill, but one that will benefit you throughout your schooling. It will also heighten your appreciation for writing. This is why you're being asked to keep a reading journal.

Some of the journal entries are directed towards exercises in the book. Others ask you to pay attention to specific qualities of a work, whether it be a published essay or a student sample (there are four of them in the final section). For example, you might study a piece for its use of transitions or to define its tone. In other words, you're writing about the writing, which will help you become attentive to these elements in your own work. It will also make you a more sophisticated reader.

So, go on an essay reading binge, starting now! It's up to you to seek out a broad range of essays, to introduce yourself to a variety of styles and approaches. Don't be limited to reading only the popular 19th century writers such as Emerson and Thoreau (though you don't want to miss them!). An anthology of essays is as close as your local library. Be sure to read contemporary pieces as well. Most magazines feature essayists. *Newsweek* runs a wonderful feature called "My Turn," which presents a new author each week. Also, find different kinds of essays. Don't always read persuasive pieces, for example. Look for personal essays, meditations on landscapes, travel pieces, historical essays, satirical essays, and so forth.

If you commit yourself to the reading journal, you will develop the depth of critical thought needed to fully appreciate the range of styles and ideas involved in essay writing. This is a worthwhile reward! Finally, have fun with it! Share your favorite works with your peers and your teacher. Feel free to embellish your reading journal with photos, drawings, and so on.

The Golden Rule:
Show—Don't Tell

It has been said that to truly digest new information a person must hear it upwards of two hundred times. If there is one principle of good writing that is worth repeating hundreds of times, it's this:

BE ILLUSTRATIVE

This could be translated into a phrase you've probably heard: *show, don't tell*. Writing teachers have been preaching this rule forever; writers will tell you it is the hallmark of their craft. While writing a story or poem, it can come naturally; after all, you're filling your story with events, your poem with images. Yet when it comes to essays, students have a hard time being illustrative. Why is this? What exactly do we mean by being illustrative?

When you watch a movie, you are presented with images, events, conflicts. You are not *told* what is happening. Imagine sitting down in a movie theater, eating your popcorn, and then seeing the director appear on the screen. He speaks: "This movie is an exciting action thriller about a team of climbers that get trapped in a snow cave. It's a story of courage and the resilience of the human spirit." It goes on like this for two hours. Yikes! You would walk out of the theater, wouldn't you? You don't want to be told about the movie—you want to be shown.

Let's extend the analogy to an essay about the Civil War. The thesis statement is that women and children in rural areas are the forgotten casualties of the Civil War. Here's a sample passage:

> In 1861, the Civil War began. It was a battle between the Union and the Confederacy. There was a lot of bloodshed and sorrow. The women and children left alone on rural farms suffered a lot. They were the forgotten casualties of the Civil War.

Now, there's nothing "wrong" with this passage. Mechanically, it's sound and it communicates some facts. But is it compelling? Does it invite the reader to continue reading the essay instead of simply picking up a book on the same subject? Aren't we presented with sweeping generalities, facts delivered in a factual manner? This brings us to an important point: *You must bring your intelligence and creativity to bear on the topic.* When we write creatively, we strive for personality, originality—our own voice. Why not strive for this in an essay? This brings us to our second "commandment":

ESSAYS ARE CREATIVE

Two hundred times! We must learn that essay writing requires imagination, order, and subtlety. Most of us have limited essay writing to a chore. Yes, it is demanding, but it can also be more fun that we think. Here's another version of our Civil War paragraph:

> In 1861, soldiers bombarded Fort Sumter, and the war between the Union and the Confederacy began. For the next four years, muskets fired and young men from all over the United States died on lonesome fields. Yet in rural farms, women and children often remained to fend for themselves, fearing the ruthless looting of undisciplined soldiers. Many were left widowed and orphaned. These are the forgotten casualties of the Civil War.

This paragraph presents the same information, only with a lot more color. Is this writing creative? Of course! The imagery and dramatic tone add spirit to a passage that was encyclopedia dry.

Now, this isn't to say that your essays have to be dense with imagery or patched with narrative. After all, there is a major difference between stories and essays. Depending on the kind of essay you're writing, you will need to clarify ideas, add supporting points, and so forth. You may have to work with abstractions rather than concrete images. Still, you can do so by being illustrative.

Importantly, in most essays you have to make declarative statements. You will have to come out and say, "The women and children who also endured the horrors of death and depravity have become the forgotten casualties of the Civil War." Fair enough. It's a strong and general statement. Now the writer must prove the point. How? Through details, through illustration. Hence, our third writing law:

EARN YOUR GENERALITIES

In the sample paragraphs above, notice how the same thesis statement, "women and children were the forgotten casualties of the Civil War," is more powerful when it comes after a series of engaging details. In the second passage, the statement was *earned* because the ideas that warranted it were brought to life. In another essay, these details might consist of statistics, direct quotes, or compelling facts—the key is that they illustrate the point.

The following list offers a few strategies that will lead to more illustrative writing. These are only a few approaches. As your writing style develops, you'll find creative touches all your own.

(1) **Be specific**. This applies to word choice, development, and tone. Suppose I'm writing a paper about the dangers of gambling:

> Slot machines, even more than other forms of gambling, are especially addictive and evil. People sit there and think they have a chance to win, but the odds are heavily against them. Before they know it, a lot of time and money has been wasted.

Now let's color it in:

> Dropping coins in slot machines, even more than playing Blackjack or craps, is insidious and addictive. The slot junkies, typically the middle aged and elderly, sit on their stools and hope for a triple lemon. But the odds are stacked: maybe one in fifty pulls is a winner. Before they know it, these unfortunates have lost thousands of irreplaceable hours and dollars to the slot machines.

The words are more exact, the imagery more illustrative, and the tone more energetic. It shows instead of tells! Most importantly, the second example does a better job of persuading the reader.

(2) **Look for analogies**. There are many ways to state something, and some are more stirring than others. As a writer, look for creative ways to bring statistics and facts to life. For example, let's take a look at a cultural icon:

> In houses all over the United States, little girls covet their Barbies, which cost between $12 and $150 apiece. The amount of money spent on these dolls is incredible, and that's not to mention the money spent on Barbie's clothes!

Okay. We get the picture, but maybe there's another way to put this that takes us beyond the abstraction of such high numbers:

> In houses all over the United States, little girls covet their Barbies, which cost between $12 and $150 apiece. We could buy groceries for a month on a Barbie collector's budget! Now imagine adding the cost of Barbie's expensive clothing. We don't spend that kind of money on our own wardrobes!

The creative comparison makes it more concrete, doesn't it? The reader is more likely to be shocked by the money spent on Barbies.

(3) **When it's appropriate, get personal.** While we're taught not to use the 'I' in an essay, if handled well, there is room for it. Anecdotes, for example, are very popular. Say you're writing about the wonders of the New England fall. The paper is meant to celebrate the season while explaining why the leaves change color. It would be wholly appropriate to begin your essay with a personal account:

> When I was seven years old, my aunt picked me up from the Hartford Airport. It was my first visit to New England. As we drove down highway 91 and looked over the Pioneer Valley, I thought I was dreaming: The valley was covered with trees swirling with shades of red, green, and brown. I thought I was in a Monet painting.

As long as the narrative stopped here, it would be a lovely segue into the paper.

WRITING PRACTICE

(A) Adding more illustration, rewrite the three following paragraphs.

> (1) The pollution in our city is pretty bad, especially in the summer months when we're asked to stay inside to avoid breathing the smoggy air. Thankfully, city officials are trying hard to get something done.

> (2) The band performed one of its best concerts ever. The way the crowd was moved was a testimony to the effectiveness of the performance. I know that the band will continue to sell out its concerts throughout the tour.

> (3) In *Romeo and Juliet* the lessons we learn are many. There is enough sadness and tragedy in the story to allow for reconciliation between the Capulets and Montagues. Romeo and Juliet really loved each other, so much so that they were willing to die for their love.

(B) When you're done, rewrite "Class Size" on the following page. Beginning with the title, color the piece by adding specifics and illustrations. Your goal, remember, is to earn your generalities.

READING CONNECTION

As you read essays in the coming months, look for examples of illustrative writing. Are the generalities earned? Are there passages that are particularly compelling or especially boring perhaps? Enter your responses in your reading journal.

Class Size

Class size is a real problem in our public schools. There are simply too many students. There are sometimes 40 or more in each class. In such an environment, how are students supposed to get the attention they need to learn? How is a teacher supposed to be able to look through her students' work with care?

There are so many benefits to having smaller class size. The teachers have the time to give more attention to individual students, for example. In a classroom of 40 students, there are too many distractions. Students are more likely to get involved in side conversations than in a lesson.

Small class size would also help students socially. When the class is packed with students, the classroom atmosphere is rather scattered, making it difficult to get to know other kids. Also, if a student is shy, he or she is less likely to ask the teacher questions or reach out to his or her peers.

Reducing class size would also benefit teachers. For example, the teachers would have less work to take home with them once school lets out. Considering how hard teachers work, they could certainly use a little more time to themselves. This would make them refreshed for the next day, and more able to give the students the attention they need.

Fortunately, some steps have been taken to reduce class size in the early grades. All of us should continue to pressure the people in charge to make smaller class size a reality in all grades. Not only will this change benefit students and teachers, but the country as a whole, too.

Style, Tone, Audience

When we listen to Beethoven, we say he's a Romantic composer. When we see a Renoir painting, we talk about his impressionistic style. Clearly, achieving a style is central to any artist, whether she be a fashion designer or a pianist. But does style apply to writing? If it does, then how do we define it? Do *you* have one? Does style matter in essay writing in particular?

It absolutely matters. In fact, along with your tone, your style adds flavor to your voice and texture to your writing. And yes, you have a writing style! We all do, though our own style may differ depending on the kind of writing we're doing.

So, what determines writing style? Let's find out by beginning with a simple exercise. Referring to a book or essay that you love, answer each of the questions below. These are only starting points; but they will give you an idea of what is meant by a writer's style. You'll soon discover that an accomplished writer's style, like her tone, will be hard to pin down. After all, voice and tone are the result of years of writing and discovery.

- Are there lots of adjectives? Are the verbs strong?
- Are the sentences long or short? Does their structure vary? What structure does the writer prefer?
- Are the paragraphs long or short? Does their structure vary?
- What sort of *rhythm* is achieved within the sentences and paragraphs?
- What kind of language does the author use? Formal? Informal? Is the vocabulary elevated? Is there slang?
- Are the descriptions highly detailed or more general?
- What kind of pacing does the writer achieve? Leisurely? Urgent?
- Does the writer use devices such as imagery, metaphor or symbolism?

Again, these are only some of the qualities that contribute to style. The more aggressively you look into it, the more you'll discover.

TONE

It's impossible to separate a writer's style from his tone. Yet while the style is often definable, the tone is more illusive. Let's explore it.

When we talk about someone's tone of voice, we're not referring to what she says as much as *how* she says it. Suppose you're standing in line at the grocery store and the gentleman behind you says, "Can I skip ahead of you? Your cart is full and I'm only buying a candy bar." How will you take this? It depends, doesn't it? If he asks you insistently, assuming it's your duty as a thoughtful citizen to switch places in line, and if you don't you're violating some code of conduct, you're less likely to respond, right? If his tone is gentle and polite, you'll probably be willing.

These same laws apply to essay writing: Your tone will help determine how your material affects your reader. This isn't to say that an angry or insistent or negative tone is undesirable. It may be wholly appropriate. Always remember, however, that part of your style is your tone, and *your writing has a tone.*

Return now to the work you used to define style. Referring to the list below, spend a few minutes trying to define the author's tone. Keep in mind that this is an abbreviated list. It's likely you'll have to settle on a combination of these.

- happy
- formal
- informal
- rushed
- intense
- insistent
- angry
- humorous
- sarcastic
- defeated
- lazy
- dramatic
- elevated
- quiet
- gentle
- mysterious
- cryptic
- self-deprecating

It's not easy to define, is it? That's because you're hearing the writer's *voice,* which is the result of years of development. There might be one word that captures the tone perfectly, but you'll have to wrestle to find it.

Now, why does tone matter to your writing? How does it apply to essays? To answer this, let's take a look at the question of audience.

AUDIENCE

Before beginning an essay, always ask yourself to whom you are directing your writing. In other words, who is your audience? What is the right tone for your audience? If you're writing an editorial to your local paper, for example, you want to establish a tone that will be assertive yet reach the general readership. Going a step further, you still have to ask yourself how assertive you want to be; if you come across as too angry or accusatorial, you run the risk of alienating the reader. (This is touched on more in the essay writing section.) If you're writing a research paper on the fluctuation of the walking strides of alligator lizards in the northern reaches of Los Angeles County, your intended audience is unlikely to be moved by a highly poetic tone. What if you're composing a speech to be delivered before the local Girl Scouts? You'll want to achieve a friendly, conversational tone, right?

The question of audience extends beyond tone. For example, what level of vocabulary would be suitable? What kind of humor, if any, would be tasteful? Are there some phrases or anecdotes that may be offensive? Are you using content that will reach the audience? Haven't we all read essays making references to historical figures or other celebrities that we don't recognize? (Ever heard of Jimmy Durante or Golda Meyer?) Perhaps we weren't the intended audience.

AUDIENCE EXERCISE

(A) Let's practice identifying the intended audience of two popular periodicals: *Reader's Digest* and *The New Yorker*. You can find both of these at your local library. Compare and contrast a few articles from each. Look at the writing styles, the level of vocabulary, the nature of the content, and so forth. Also, notice the advertising. Can you describe what kind of audience is most likely to read each magazine?

(B) This is an amusing way to illustrate the importance of audience. You can do this exercise on your own or in a group. First, decide on **one** essay topic for the whole group. Let's say you choose "The importance of eating your green vegetables." Everyone has to write a one page essay on that topic. The catch is that each person should be assigned a different audience. This can be determined by a teacher, or chosen randomly from strips of paper.

So, one person will be writing to a prime minister, while another will be addressing a group of sixth graders. The texture of the essays will be quite different! When you're done, read the papers out loud.

STYLE AND TONE EXERCISES

(A) Using the lists on pages 8 and 9, study the style and tone of a few pieces of your own writing. Can you see tendencies? Do your style and tone change? If so, why?

(B) You can do this exercise with a partner, too. Simply exchange some work and try to determine each other's writing style. It's possible that your partner will see something you overlooked.

(C) Study the style and tone of several published essays. Describe them in your reading journal.

Introductions and Conclusions: Bookends with a Punch

When you begin to read an essay, chances are you'll know within the opening paragraph whether or not you want to continue. If you complete the piece, the final paragraph will likely remain with you; or if it's a dud, it might sap the energy from the rest of the essay. Colorful, effective introductions and conclusions are essential to the essay.

INTRODUCTIONS

An attractive introduction does two things: It grabs the reader's interest, and it establishes the tone and intention of the paper. Too often introductions consist of a series of statements and generalities. Suppose you were reading a persuasive paper that warns of the dangers of teenage smoking. It opens like this:

> All over the United States more and more young people are smoking cigarettes. Doctors will tell you that smoking is very hazardous to your health. So it doesn't really make sense to keep smoking, does it? Teenagers think it's cool, but what they don't know is that they're in danger of becoming victims of a life threatening addiction. In the following essay I will explain the dangers of smoking, especially in regards to teenagers. I will examine the causes, health risks and psychological dangers involved.

This is an informative, clear introduction. There's nothing "wrong" with it, but does it grab the reader? If you were tempted to smoke, or knew someone who smoked, would this introduction make you want to read on? Compare it to this one:

> You come home and wash your hands in hot water, scrubbing them with soap. But the harsh tobacco smell remains. You brush your teeth several times, but your smile is still stained with yellow and brown. Yet what you can see and smell is nothing compared to what you can't see: the black tar building up in your fifteen year old lungs, and the minutes, hours, and days you're robbing from your life by smoking cigarettes.

Notice the strategy here. The writer opens with a storyline—a gripping, suspenseful illustration—making you want to read on. This is called a "hook," which serves to grab the reader right away. That isn't to say that you must have a fantastic, dramatic introduction. As long as you're able to pique the reader's interest, you have done your job. There are many possibilities, of course. We could have used statistics: "Three thousand teenagers begin smoking every day" would certainly work. Also, notice that the writer doesn't have to announce her intention in the essay—it's implicit. Nor does she explain how the paper is outlined. Unless there's a good reason for it—to clarify a complex structure, for example—let the paper unfold naturally.

CONCLUSIONS

Many students find writing conclusions to be the most difficult part of the essay. "How do I end it?" they ask. The answer is simple: Make it as stirring and interesting as the introduction. Let's illustrate our point. Here is one conclusion to our anti-smoking paper:

> In conclusion, smoking is a terrible and dangerous habit. As I have shown, smoking causes cancer and heart disease, not to mention tooth decay and a declined sense of smell and taste. It is very addictive, containing additives that make the smoker dependent. So, if you're thinking of lighting up because your friends do, think again.

Like our first introduction, this conclusion is clear. It wraps up the paper and sends the reader off with an assertive punch. Again, there's nothing "wrong" with it. But as active writers, we can make it better. Now let's compare it with another version:

> After thirty years of sheltering himself from the realities of smoking, the patient learns that he has lung cancer. He thinks back to his teenage years and the first time he lit up with friends. He remembers brushing his teeth and washing his hands to try to hide the smell from his parents. He remembers the many times his friends and family told him to quit, the times he laughed it off, saying, "We all gotta go some time." Only now he realizes that "some time" might be closer than he thinks. So the next time you're offered a cigarette, think again: this patient could be you.

We have an illustrative, dramatic closing. By alluding to the introduction, the writer has established a continuity and sense of structure. This is called the **envelope strategy**, which involves opening and closing with a similar image or theme. Notice also that the writer doesn't use the standard signpost "In conclusion." This is a handy phrase, but it's predictable and rather dull. Nor does the writer restate the points of the essay. If the paper is clear and well structured, and if the voice and style are well established, typically there isn't a need to restate what was just discussed.

INTRODUCTION AND CONCLUSION EXERCISES

(A) Adding punch and color, rewrite the introduction and conclusion below.

Introduction:

Dolphins are beautiful sea creatures. Throughout the centuries and throughout the world they have been revered. There are stories of these graceful creatures saving humans from drowning and even communicating with them. In the following essay, I will explore the rich history of these magnificent sea mammals, looking into mythology and factual events.

Conclusion:

As you have seen, dolphins are exceptional sea mammals. From the seas of Japan to the shores of Malibu, the many stories and myths about them are remarkable. So the next time you are near the ocean, look for the majestic leaps of these wonderful creatures. You never know when you might have a magic moment.

(B) Let's have some fun practicing introductions and conclusions. Choose three of the following topics, and write a predictable introduction and conclusion. Then follow it up by an attractive pair. If you want, you can do this with a partner. Simply exchange introductions and conclusions for rewriting.

- Prayer in public school
- The benefits of exercise
- How to talk to your teenager
- Personal computers: a curse or a blessing?
- The history of my town
- The greatest board game in the world

Paragraphing: Units of Thought

Most of us are familiar with the most basic paragraph structure: the topic sentence followed by supporting points and a conclusion. While learning to develop your ideas and to keep your paragraph cohesive, it's a helpful structure. However, it is elemental and it has its limits, especially when you're writing a longer piece. By relying on a uniform model of paragraphing, you run the risk of monotony, of adopting a sing-songy drone to your material. Again, there's nothing wrong with starting at the beginning. Now it's time to see what other possibilities there are in paragraphing.

First, we should ask ourselves a few simple questions: What is a paragraph? What purpose does it serve? When is a new one needed?

A paragraph is a unit of thought which merits its own separate identity. Each sentence within it is part of that identity. By isolating ideas, paragraphs help create emphasis, contrast, and, as we'll see, variety. Most of the time you'll know when a new paragraph is needed: One unit of thought has reached its conclusion, and is in need of further development or contrast. At other times it's a matter of style and judgment, and this is where our interest lies; for like words and sentences, paragraphs are malleable, an expression of the writer's style.

Who's to say, for example, that a paragraph can't be one sentence long? If it has enough dramatic effect, if it gives the essay the punch it needs, why not? Can a paragraph be a page long? Of course, as long as there's a reason for it. *Let the content of the piece instruct you how to structure the paragraphs.* In this sense, paragraphs are like sentences: They work best when they work kinetically, creating sparks of meaning. This is when paragraphing, like the rest of the composition process, is a creative act.

PARAGRAPHING EXERCISES

(A) This exercise will help us see some of the possibilities in paragraphing. Suppose you have completed your first draft on the ever popular Annual Snail Race sponsored by your local fire department. The paper is well structured, showing how the snails' speed is determined by a variety of factors, including shell shape, eating habits, and so on. You describe the thrilling race and explain that the proceeds are donated to charity.

For the sake of illustration, let's say you've written the paper without paragraphs. Read the following passage, then mark the places you want a new paragraph. (A paragraph mark looks like this: ¶) Try it a few times, experimenting with different breaks. Notice how they affect the meaning of the passage. Is there an opportunity for a one sentence dramatic paragraph? Are there some obvious breaking points? When you're done, compare your choices with a partner's.

The Wet Falls Annual Snail Race picked up speed this year with a whopping three thousand plus spectators. The contestants brought their slugs from as far as Lomita County, three hundred miles away. This year's favorite, Slimy Charley, dropped out of the race when, during training, he slid into a pocket of ivy and was never found again. The front runner is now Turbo the Terrestrial Mollusk, known for his explosive bursts of speed. By now you must be asking: How do you get a snail to race? What makes them go fast? Well, you'll be surprised to know that it's simply a matter of love and encouragement and, yes, food. Contrary to popular opinion, snails are not unfeeling pests with no brains. As snail owner Mary Jones-Perot says, "I play music—Mozart only—for Rockin' Rebecca every day before practice. If I forget to play the music, or if Beethoven happens to slip in, she won't come out of her shell." Mary's husband and competitor, the famous French snailman, Marques Perot, actually constructed a snail house for Pierre, his champion runner. "When I built the house, Pierre started winning," he says proudly. "He ran the ten foot dash in under fifteen minutes," he adds with a smile. Now, snails can't race on love and encouragement alone. The promise of a leafy green at the end of the race never hurts. Sensitive trainers will figure out their snails' diets before a race, and rub a scented trail from start to finish. But these tactics are not without controversy. Maria and Raymond Ortiz, owners of Gooey, last year's runner up, complained that Slimy Charley's strongly scented trail buried the smell of dark chocolate, Gooey's favorite. This lead to stricter rules on scenting a snail's path. While all this competition is quite serious, the proceeds of the race go to local charities. This gets the community involved. There's a raffle, food booths, and of course, the $100.00 contest entry fee. The winner gets a gift certificate from Jim's Manure and Feed. So you can see that the Wet Falls Annual Snail Race is for a good cause, and studying it is an education in the depth, character, and speed of snails.

(B) Find an on-line essay, or scan a published essay into your computer. After duplicating the essay, have someone eliminate all the paragraphs so that it reads as a block. Now, locate the best places for paragraph breaks and compare your choices to the writer's. Don't assume your breaks are "wrong"—it may be a matter of style. What is important is that you understand the choices and develop your own paragraphing sensibility.

READING CONNECTION

Study the paragraph choices in a few published essays. How long are the paragraphs? Do they vary? What instructed the writer's choices? Are the paragraphs effective? Enter your impressions in your reading journal.

Brainstorming to Drafting

Even enthusiastic writers have experienced the frustration of sitting in front of a blank page (or computer screen), waiting for a topic to come. Suddenly the white space appears to be an impenetrable void. "How will I possibly fill this page?" you ask yourself. Let's look at a few strategies that help generate ideas and jump start the writing process.

Whichever type of essay you're writing, the topics are limitless. Then why is it difficult for so many of us to decide on something? Why is "I don't know what to write about" such a common complaint in writing classes? What can help?

If you're struggling to find a topic, realize that most likely you're experiencing a psychological roadblock. By deciding on a topic, you're committing to hours of work and you're striking a lot of other possibilities. It may sound too simple, but perhaps the best advice is to *decide* ! Ask yourself: If someone offered you $100.00 to find a topic within ten minutes, would you? Probably! So, decide!

Students often want to change their topics halfway through the paper; there will be a time when you hit a wall, and it gets difficult to write. At this point the tendency is to retreat and to think that another topic will be easier. Maybe, but doubtful.

BRAINSTORMING

Whether you need help finding or developing a topic, **brainstorming** is a useful technique. You might be familiar with how this works: Take a piece of construction paper and jot down *all the thoughts* that come to mind about your topic. Flood the paper with ideas, opinions, and details, even if they seem unrelated. You never know when the peripheral idea might lead you to wonderful details. For now set aside rules of grammar, spelling, and so forth, and *keep going*. After a while you should have a rich landscape of ideas before you.

A related strategy is called **mind mapping**. Like brainstorming, mind mapping invites a free flow of ideas, but it goes a step further in both form and content. Look at our sample mind map on the following page (it's in its infancy, of course). Notice that the topic is circled in the center of the paper. From that point, the web of ideas begins to form. Ideas branch off of ideas and connect across to others. Some find it helpful to embellish the mind map with drawings, quotes—whatever gives more life to the ideas. You might find an added bonus here: By linking ideas and making them colorful, mind maps often suggest structure.

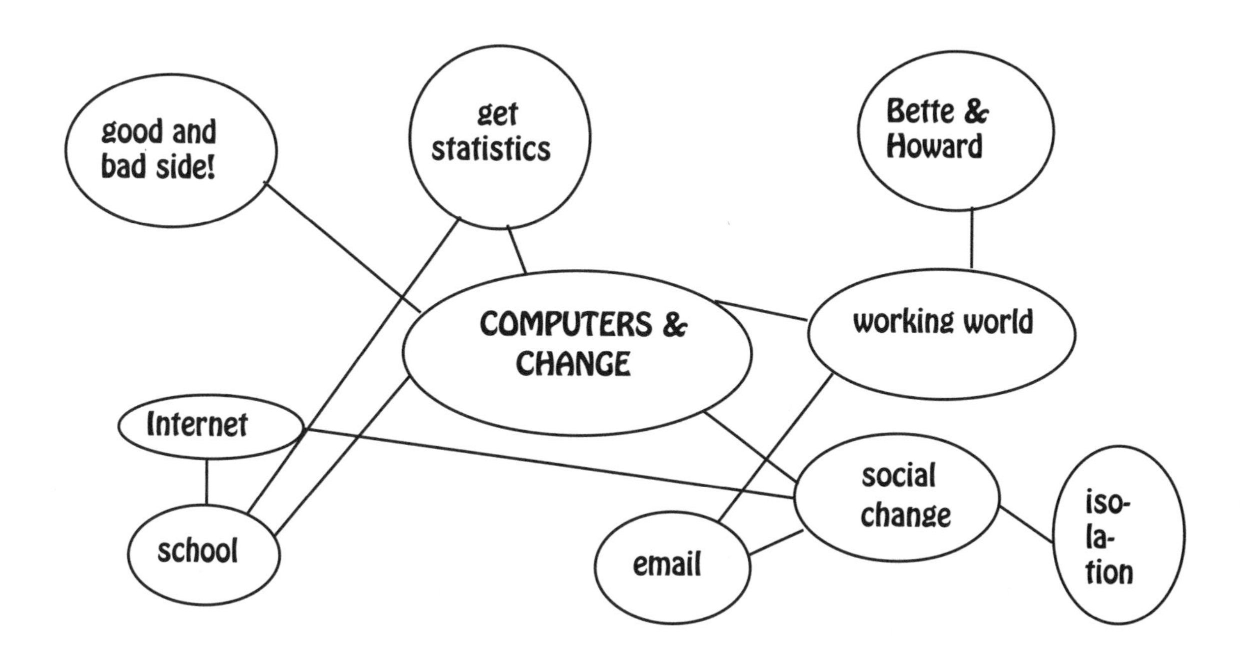

OUTLINING

There are a variety of approaches to outlining, but in principle they are all the same. By providing a skeleton to the paper, an outline ensures that your ideas will be ordered, balanced and logical. Students who try to write papers without a set structure usually produce unbalanced, scattered pieces. We can liken it to building a home. Architects draw up blueprints before building; otherwise the living room might end up smaller than the kitchen. While these same planning principles apply to writing, students often resist them, claiming they're not needed, that they're a waste of time. Actually, the opposite is usually true. By outlining your paper, you will save time.

In a good outline, each idea is related, adding depth to the main topic or thesis. You can achieve this balance in a number of ways, some of which are discussed in the essay writing section. For now, we will review the **formal outline**.

Using your brainstorm or mindmap as a starting point, begin by stating your **thesis**, which asserts what your paper is about, what it is setting out to prove. Everything in your outline, therefore, must in some way relate to your thesis statement. The next step is to divide your piece into **main topics**. Now, find at least two or three **subtopics** that support your main topics. It's important that the subtopics don't overlap, and that they are broad enough to require support themselves. For each of these, provide **supporting points**. Depending on the breadth of those points, you may have **details** for each. These supporting points and details are the heart of your paper, the illustrative examples, statistics, and so forth, that bring your thesis to life.

Here is a model of a formal outline drawn from our mind map. Notice how the ideas flow logically, moving from general to specific. Keep in mind that this is only a model. Some of your sections might require more or fewer subtopics and details.

Thesis Statement: The personal computer is changing the American way of life.

I. Main Topic..........Work
- A. Subtopic..........more employees work at computers all day
  - 1. Supporting point..........new jobs require computer skills
    - a. Detail..........examples of computer related jobs
    - b. Detail..........statistics on computer related jobs
    - c. Detail..........want ads in paper
- B. Subtopic..........more people work from home
  - 1. Supporting point..........true for both company workers and home-based businesses
    - a. Detail..........statistics on people working from home
    - b. Detail..........interview with Bette and Howard (home-based)
    - c. Detail..........interview with Sally (company)

II. Main topic.....................Social Change
- A. Subtopic..........more communication
  - 1. Supporting point..........email and Internet allow fast communication
    - a. Detail..........international chat room
    - b. Detail..........more expedient than "snail mail"
    - c. Detail..........cultural and racial barriers dropped
- B. Subtopic..........less communication
  - 1. Supporting point..........people spending more time isolated in front of the computer.
    - a. Detail..........replaces family time
    - b. Detail..........creates illusion of relationship
    - c. Detail..........statistics

III. Main topic.....................Education
- A. Subtopic..........schools
  - 1. Supporting point..........learning modified by computers
    - a. Detail..........the use of the Internet for research
    - b. Detail..........word processors in every classroom
    - c. Detail..........an increase in graphic design and other computer related electives
- B. Subtopic..........home
  - 1. Supporting point..........a huge increase in home education
    - a. Detail..........homeschoolers using virtual classrooms
    - b. Detail..........universities using virtual classrooms
    - c. Detail..........more information and learning at your fingertips

From the look of this outline you can tell this essay will primarily highlight the positive aspects of computers while embracing the complexity of the issue. If this had been a persuasive paper highlighting the negative side of the computer age, then your outline would have reflected that bias. As it is, you can see how helpful it is to have an outline as a starting point. The writer is at ease with her structure and can now get on to the business of writing.

DRAFTING YOUR PAPER

As we said, the first sentence is often the hardest. Here are a few tips that you might find helpful when beginning your first draft.

(1) **Remember that it's your first draft**. Too often students feel pressured to write the perfect piece the first time around. Usually this is because they consider the paper to be done after the first draft. Experienced writers will tell you that when they finish the first draft, their work has just begun! So, while you want to be careful, let your ideas flow smoothly, without the butcher's knife of editing. If you've paced yourself well, there will be time to revise. So, START WRITING! In fact, you might find it helpful to simply start scribbling *anything* on the page. That first step breaks the ice. By filling in the white page, you start to have concrete ideas on paper. You'll be surprised how helpful this is.

(2) **Skip the introduction and begin with the body of the paper**. Introductions are hard to write. Like conclusions, they express the overall spirit and intention of the paper. So, the perfect illustrative opening might come clear only after your paper unfolds. And by beginning with the body of the paper, you're onto something concrete right away. You start getting stuff down and gathering momentum.

(3) **Give yourself a good chunk of time every time you write**. Writing is no different than playing baseball or piano: You have to warm up. It might take you ten minutes just to get settled, and another ten for your thoughts to start to flow. If you allowed yourself thirty minutes to write, then you'll complete an astonishing ten minutes of work! By giving yourself a couple of hours for each shift, you'll get more done, and when it's all added up, you'll spend less time doing it.

(4) **Follow your outline**. In the drafting process there's always a danger of losing touch with your outline. This usually happens when the writing is going well, for the writer is susceptible to getting overexcited and may begin to digress.

REVISING YOUR PAPER

"Good writing," said the author Roald Dahl, "is rewriting." To perform flawlessly on the balance beam, the gymnast has to first deal with falling and trying again; to sail a boat, the captain has to play with the wind until tacking becomes instinctive. This principle of practice applies to writing; in fact, it applies to *every sentence.*

Unfortunately, many students consider their first draft to be their only draft, forgoing even the most rudimentary proofreading efforts. While this negligence is regrettable, what's worse is that the student is missing the fun (yes, fun!) and satisfaction of rewriting a piece. To see sentences come together fluidly, to say something just right, is deeply rewarding. *Unless you push yourself to get to this step, it won't come.* Strive to be an objective reader of your own work—a difficult and lasting challenge! Most of us tend to read what we wish was on the paper rather than what is actually printed.

So, assuming you have your first draft before you, it's time to take it slowly, to chisel away at the sentences that read awkwardly, to find the right word, to economize the fluffy phrases. Here are a few tips:

(1) **Edit first, then rewrite**. While everyone has his own method, you'll probably find the revision process smoother by first getting down to the nitty-gritty of editing. After editing, you can conduct your rewrite in an orderly manner. This divides your work into manageable pieces and helps you focus on one element at a time.

(2) **Edit in spurts**. Unlike the drafting process, concentrated editing is best done in short shifts, generally no more than half-an-hour. The demands of looking critically at your own work requires lots of attention and honesty. When you begin to tire, you tend to be a little kinder to yourself than the piece merits.

(3) **Know when to add, and when to subtract**. The longing for a paper to be done keeps us from cutting and whittling, and from adding. But we have to stay true to the paper. You'll probably find more opportunities for eliminating than for embellishing. We will attend to this in detail in the next section of the book.

A WORD ON TITLES

At some point in the drafting process, you want to come up with a good title. Titles are important, for they can give your paper momentum and focus while attracting the reader. A bad title has the reverse effect.

Let's say you're writing about the history of the kite. Which title sounds better: "The History of the Kite," or "Flying Kites through the Ages"? The latter sounds better, doesn't it? Of course, if you wanted to take a chance at humor, you could risk "Go Fly a Kite"!

A word of caution: Don't go overboard on titles. While you want to interest the reader and grab the spirit of the piece, you don't want to compromise clarity. "The Tail of the Boxed Aerial Floater," while poetic, is a bit much!

Sentence Fluidity

Identifying Awkward Sentences

In this next section, we will devote considerable time to identifying and writing smooth, attractive sentences. Sentences, after all, are the lifeblood of composition. You might have the greatest ideas in the world, but if your sentences stumble along, they will fail to communicate the depth of your thoughts.

We will begin by identifying some of the more common habits that get in the way of good writing. As you'll see, in some cases we will be dealing with identifiable grammatical errors. Primarily, however, we will highlight less obvious tendencies that inhibit an author's readability.

Good writing has to be smooth, active, and economized. While it doesn't have to be "easy reading," the sentences must make sense and be cohesive. This cohesiveness is most often compromised by awkward sentence structures. These structures are often remedied by practicing **economy of expression**. Once you start whittling away at words and phrases, you'll find that your writing is smoother and has more impact. Let's begin with some identifiable constructs that create awkward or illogical sentences.

(1) We proofread our papers for spelling and punctuation errors, but we often forget to check for errors in sensibility and logic. Look at this sentence:

-In his endeavor to make better coffee, it tasted like water.

Can you see why this doesn't make sense? We know what the writer is trying to say, but that doesn't make the sentence any smoother or more grammatically sound. Nor can it give this sentence a clear subject. Did "the endeavor" make the coffee bad, or did "he"? The pronoun "it" suggests that it was indeed "the endeavor," but the way the sentence is constructed, the subject should be "he". This kind of flaw is called a **mixed construction**, which takes place when a writer connects phrases or clauses that don't work together logically. It's like putting a roof where a wall belongs. When deciding whether a sentence is fluid, trust your ear. If something seems off, it probably is! By adding a subject to our example, a logical relationship between clauses emerges:

-In his endeavor to make better coffee, he made it taste like water.

Isolating a sentence helps to highlight its awkwardness. In a sea of sentences, however, it won't be so easy to target. That's why we have to revise aggressively.

(2) Another common mistake involves the **misuse of conjunctions and subordinates.** Conjunctions determine the direction of the sentence, either by strengthening a statement or by contrasting it. Subordinates establish a relationship between clauses in a sentence (for a review, see page 46). Be careful with these shifts in meaning or you'll end up with sentences like these:

> -While the historical building, old and decaying, will not be torn down. [misuse of subordinate]
> -The reason the building, though old and decaying, will not be torn down is because it is a historical monument. [misuse of conjunction]

In the first sentence, "while" sets up a relationship between ideas that never unfolds. It's a fragment! The second example is trickier. The conjunction "because" cannot function as an adjective or a noun. Besides that, these sentences sound wrong, don't they? Here are a couple of alternatives:

> -While the historical building, old and decaying, will not be torn down, it will be renovated.
> -The reason the building, though old and decaying, will not be torn down is clear: It is a historical monument.

(3) Another mistake in logic appears in the **misplaced** and **dangling modifier**. Though you have probably covered this, it's worth reviewing briefly in the light of sentence construction and revision. What's wrong with the following sentences?

> -As she sewed all night on the front porch, the moon passed over Ma.
> -Having shoveled dirt all day, there was a hole ten feet deep.

In the first sentence, either the moon knows how to sew or we have a problem! This is a misplaced modifier. In the second example, there is no recipient of the modifier "Having shoveled dirt all day." Thus, we have a dangling modifier. Let's correct the sentences:

> -The moon passed over Ma as she sewed all night on the front porch.
> -Having shoveled dirt all day, we had a hole ten feet deep.

(4) Another awkward practice is the use of "where" and "when" to define things. Sometimes this is appropriate, but not usually. Look at these sentences:

> -A piñata is when you break a papier-mâché creature and lots of candy falls out.
> -I know a lot of adventure movies where the main character is overshadowed by the villain.

A piñata is not "when you break a papier-mâché creature...." A piñata is a papier-mâché creature! And are adventure movies a "where"? Both of these sentences are illogical, yet these defining strategies are common. Here they are again:

-A piñata is a papier-mâché creature. When it breaks open, lots of candy falls out.
-I know a lot of adventure movies in which the main character is overshadowed by the villain.

(5) As you can see, there's a reason that sentences become awkward. Above all else, sentences need to be clear and logical. Sometimes, faulty logic is less obvious. Look at these examples:

-The cold wind stuffed up Carl's nose.
-Water pollution has become a state priority.

Most of us would read these without asking for clarity. But can "cold wind" actually "stuff up" someone's nose. With some imagination, maybe! Certainly water pollution is *not* a priority! That would be most unfortunate. Let's make these sentences clear:

-After Carl was exposed to the cold wind, his nose became stuffed.
-Eliminating water pollution has become a state priority.

Some sentences aren't easy to fix. If you've exhausted your possibilities, if you've restructured the sentence and can't get it right, it's time to *say it differently*. Don't revise the sentence—rewrite it. This in turn may affect the relationship to the neighboring sentences, and to the whole paragraph—so be sure to reread the material carefully.

EXERCISE: REWRITING AWKWARD SENTENCES

The following four exercises require you to rewrite awkward or illogical sentences. In certain cases you'll need to restructure the sentence altogether. Some of the sentences contain grammatical errors. Others may be "correct," but they simply *don't sound right*.

There is no need to complete this assignment in one sitting. Pace yourself, but take the work seriously. The benefits of being able to identify and correct awkward sentences are lasting.

Note: Consider studying some of the sentence combining strategies (pages 39-49) before completing these exercises. These strategies introduce you to a variety of sentence structures that are helpful in rewriting.

(A)

1. A lunar eclipse is where the earth moves in front of the sun, casting a shadow on the moon.

2. After being damaged by the earthquake, it took a long time to rebuild our home.

3. In my town, Spanish style houses try to blend into the landscape more than others.

4. Jumping rope with great style and speed, the crowd cheered her on.

5. In his attempt to cook the lasagna only caused it to burn to a charcoal.

6. I know so many examples of people where their friends double as their worst enemies.

7. The happiest times of life are good friendships.

8. Despite their attempts to get the people at the football game to recycle their cans and bottles, but students had to dig them out of the trash can anyway.

9. A utopia is when there is a perfect civilization.

10. In one powerful leap, the avalanche was started by the graceful mountain goat.

(B)

1. He told me that his relationship to his coach was struggling.

2. He decided not to sell his home for his children's sake.

3. When I started high school I thought I should start thinking of what I may want to do in the future as far as a profession.

4. We were discussing being rich or poor and which is the better one.

5. Another major issue in the news is about the Middle East peace process.

6. In volleyball, a spike is where a player leaps and slams the ball over the net.

7. She tells him he should pray and especially when he's uncertain about what to do in his decision.

8. Taking care of yourself before you get sick, instead of waiting until you're sick and then taking a pill to fix your problem.

9. No doubt that there is nothing that he thinks he can't do.

10. The airplane ran out of gas and then looked for a place to land.

(C)

1. He tries desperately to solve the problems that the callers have in the most surprising and honest ways.

2. As so many deer hunters use, I choose the rifle as my weapon of choice.

3. Traveling is definitely not on his list of fun, especially to big cities.

4. Call 911 is what the note says.

5. I was led by my interest in skateboarding to my decision on the type of friends I had.

6. Most people when they are in these situations experience butterflies in the stomach, nervousness, and a dry throat.

7. The explosions were bigger and more life-like, and the new scenes they added were magnificent in their blending into the movie.

8. One man even said that the low wages that they make as day laborers are still more than they would make in Mexico.

9. Looking at the photos later truly reflect the panic I was feeling.

10. Grades first through fourth were taught to me out of private school.

(D)

1. The reason his coarse brown hair stays in perfect form is because he applies handfuls of gel every morning.

2. Ernie attempts to imitate his dog's well-known curled lip, contorting his upper lip up slightly but the lower lip slides to the left.

3. Using his hand as his microphone, he sings with every word, slightly off-key, and screaming at the top of his lungs.

4. But wait! I can't stop now, ~~being as~~ I've come so far, after all.

5. I was made moody by the extreme desert heat.

6. A pulsing sensation like an electric shock, ran through her body when she felt the ~~pull~~ tug of the fishing pole ~~like an electric shock~~.

7. ~~The night grows late, and~~ the morning grows early, with it bringing the constant birds chirping and the crowing of roosters.

8. Each flake ~~being~~ is so intricate and unique, they whirled as they fell and settled into deep powdery drifts.

9. He's a bit skinny. ~~Well, more than a bit~~, a bean pole is the word, to me.

10. The lady's mind is made up of high self-esteem and many strong motivations.

Writing Versus Speaking

A lot of good writing comes across with a conversational flow, as if you were being spoken to. Yet this is also where many writers get into trouble, because there are some major differences between written and spoken English. If one's speaking patterns surface too often in one's writing, the result could be unfortunate.

(1) The most obvious example of this involves **incorrect word use**. We have patterns of speech that aren't correct. For example, many of us use "should of" and "could of," when we mean to say "should have," and "could have." Of course, "could of" is not acceptable in speaking, but it is habitual! We can draw a parallel to the words "a lot," which, when spoken, are heard as one word: *alot.*

There are words that are particular to your regional dialect. In many cases these are appropriate; in others, they are considered slang and can confuse the reader. Always ask yourself whether your reader will be able to comprehend your meaning, and also whether or not you're using the word correctly. In some cases, words become so popular that they lose their original meaning. Here are some examples:

-What a <u>wicked</u> traffic jam!
-Working at the restaurant was a <u>drag</u>.
-That was a <u>totally awesome</u> song.

Now, there is room for dialect and slang in your writing. After considering the audience, tone, and setting of your piece, if slang is appropriate, then go for it! Again, it's a matter of being conscious, of using it when it's appropriate. If you choose to use slang, then it's a writer's choice; otherwise, it's habit.

(2) Another speaking habit that surfaces in writing is the overuse of **intensifiers** and **qualifiers**. Intensifiers are words that attempt to add to the degree of meaning: *so, very, really.* If you consider it carefully, you'll probably agree that intensifiers are most often unnecessary. Here are a few examples:

-Grandma is <u>really</u> happy to see us today.
-The weather is <u>so</u> nice.
-There are <u>very</u> many gumballs in the machine.

Now, read each sentence without the intensifier. Do they lose any meaning? Are they more clear without the intensifiers? Yes, they are. Intensifiers appear so often that they compromise the precision of expression. While they are common in everyday speech, intensifiers are typically considered dead weight in writing.

Like intensifiers, **qualifiers** are common in speech but are suspect in writing, especially when they appear in abundance. Some qualifiers are particular to a region, so you might be able to identify your own. Here, the qualifiers are underlined:

-The puppy is kind of shy.
-It seems/appears that she's absent today.
-My feelings were sort of hurt by the piano teacher.
-In a sense, there's no reason to go through with the sale.
-It's just that I'm in the mood for something other than pizza.

The qualifiers help the writer avoid being definitive. Also, qualifiers usually don't have clear meanings: How can a puppy be "kind of" shy? Does that mean only when strangers are around? Is the puppy shy only half of the day? How can feelings be "sort of" hurt? Remove the qualifiers from the sentences above. Did they lose meaning? Always ask yourself whether the qualifier you're using adds meaning. If not, strike it.

Qualifiers and intensifiers can be necessary. Once again, the key is to *decide* when they are needed rather than letting them slip in habitually.

(3) A related habit of speech is the **informal transition**. Read the following paragraph, and notice how the underlined words and phrases are used to introduce a remark or to fill a pause.

> Well, the bus was empty and the driver was a clown. So, we had a lot of fun talking to him. It was a relaxing ride after a long day of packing. What I'm trying to say is that in my opinion the driver was a terrific guy. I mean, it was much better than riding in a crowded, silent bus.

Sound familiar? If you listen to yourself speak you'll probably hear some of these words and phrases. Of course, we exaggerated their use for the purpose of illustration. Notice how they serve as a pause, a way of pacing. They can be thought of as a formal alternative to the proverbial *um*. In writing, unless they are used to depict a dialect or a conversational preference, these informal transitions tend to dilute the meaning.

A note on the *I* : Students often ask about the appropriateness of using *I* in their essays. Most writers would agree that it should be used sparingly because it is implicit. Repeating "I think" or "I believe" only creates fluff and repetition. For example, "I think we should lower taxes" has the same meaning as "We should lower taxes."

WRITING PRACTICE: WRITING VERSUS SPEAKING

This is a two part assignment that requires a partner. First, each person writes one page (any subject) using a lot of qualifiers, intensifiers, informal transitions, and slang. When you're done, exchange papers and rewrite each other's pieces, eliminating the excess. You be the wordsmith and decide what's appropriate.

Word Precision

Now that you have begun to eliminate some of the "talky" elements of your writing, it's time to take a more advanced step: finding the *best* word or phrase. As you revise your paper, there will be times when a word or phrase doesn't seem right. The sentence may be fluid, but it can be better. Look at this sentence:

> -Only 25% of the citizens voted today, demonstrating their indifference towards the propositions on the ballot.

As an attentive writer, you get a little itchy when you read the word *indifference.* Hmm. There's got to be a more exact expression.

> -Only 25% of the citizens voted today, demonstrating their apathy towards the propositions on the ballot.

While *indifference* and *apathy* are synonymous, *apathy* points to a type of indifference that has to do with matters of importance. Let's look at a more poetic example:

> -The sun shone through the patchy clouds, making circles of light on the ocean.
> -The sun shone through the patchy clouds, spotlighting the ocean.

It's a matter of taste, but *spotlighting* certainly captures "making circles of light."

Once you actively seek out concise words and expressions, they become easier to find. Also, remember that a far-reaching vocabulary, while valuable, does not always equal good word choice. Actually, it can be detrimental. If you have ever read a writer who strives for the longest or most scholarly word, you've seen the danger firsthand:

> -The juxtaposition of the ideas in his dissertation created a tautology that left the audience nonplussed.

Here it is translated:

> -His ideas went around in circles, leaving the audience baffled.

The writer of the first sentence probably slogged through his thesaurus, citing every polysyllabic alternative to his words. The thesaurus is a valuable tool if it helps bring to mind words that you know, but that weren't at your fingertips. If you use words without being aware of their connotations, you risk loss of clarity.

Keep in mind that word precision is a skill that continually evolves. Once you get hooked on it, you start to discover some of the magical qualities of writing. There is deep satisfaction in finding just the right word or phrase.

PRECISION EXERCISE

Read the following passage below. Highlight the fluffy, imprecise material. Eliminate the excess qualifiers, intensifiers, informal transitions, and slang. Rewrite the passage using precise words and phrases. Feel free to embellish the content.

It would interest the reader to note that there are alot of really good places to eat in our town. In fact, I think it's commonly known that the grub at Linguini's Burgers and Fries is pretty much the best in the county for a semi fast food place. They also have these cool umbrellas with these patterns on them. It's colorful stuff. Also, don't forget about the splendid atmosphere at The Sea Captain's joint, which is placed right on the edge of this magnificent, gnarly cliff by the sea. While you eat your delicious seafood, you can look out on the great views. It's not an uncommon occurrence to see dolphin swimming around and jumping out of the water and enjoying themselves. So, there's lots to offer in the way of atmospherics there. And we also better mention the expensive but awesome L'House d'Spirit. This eating facility doesn't have a price for the food on its menu, so you know you're going to pay a lot of money for what you get. But when you taste the stuff—wow! In my opinion, it's like nothing you've ever experienced! I hope this gives you an idea of the variety of sundry and tremendous choices you have of where to eat in our town.

Quote Incorporation

Essays often rely on the skilled use of direct quotes for support. Whether you're citing material from a book, from the Internet, or from an interview, you need to thread the quote into the fabric of your essay in a smooth manner. How will you add someone else's words and maintain your own voice? How will you keep the ideas alive while incorporating quotes?

As you will see below, retaining this liveliness is primarily a matter of form and transitions, of incorporating quotes in a variety of ways. Before looking at different ways to incorporate quotes, however, remember this rule: *You must always incorporate a quote into your own writing*. If not, you have a "floating quote," which looks like this:

> -Neil Armstrong added a poetic touch when he landed on the moon. "That's one small step for man, one giant leap for mankind."

This is a timely quote. However, it must appear within the framework of the writer's words. There are several ways to do this. Using the moon example, let's examine five options for quote incorporation.

(1) **Use a colon**. The colon is used to relate the quote to the writer's words. The colon replaces the words, "Here's an example," or "Read the following." Importantly, when introducing a quote, *the colon must follow a complete sentence*:

> -Neil Armstrong added a poetic touch when he landed on the moon: "That's one small step for man, one giant leap for mankind."

(2) **Begin with the quote, then use your own words**. This strategy is self-explanatory. It might require an added "said" to segue into the rest of the information:

> -"That's one small step for man, one giant leap for mankind," said Neil Armstrong, adding a poetic touch when he landed on the moon.

(3) **Begin with your own words, then introduce the quote**. This is the reverse of the strategy above:

> -Neil Armstrong, adding a poetic touch when he landed on the moon, said, "That's one small step for man, one giant leap for mankind."

(4) **Divide the quote**. This is a more sophisticated strategy. Whether you have a long quote that you want to divide, or you want to emphasize parts of the quote, this is a good way to go. Notice how the quote is embellished:

-Neil Armstrong added a poetic touch when he landed on the moon. "That's one small step for man," he declared 250,000 miles away from Earth, "one giant leap for mankind."

(5) **Segue the quote into your sentence without using punctuation**. Notice how the quote naturally fits into the sentence. This is a good but difficult strategy. By dropping the opening "That's," the quote flows right into the meaning of the sentence:

-Neil Armstrong added a poetic touch to his moon landing when he took "one small step for man, one giant leap for mankind."

In addition to these incorporation strategies, a couple of pertinent punctuation rules should be mentioned.

(A) **When quoting a passage of four or more lines, indent the excerpt instead of using quotation marks**. This is a little tricky. By setting off a passage on its own, you are establishing that it's a long direct quote, so *you don't need quotation marks.* However, if you're quoting dialogue, as from a novel, you need the quotation marks. If it helps, remember this simple rule: When excerpting a passage of four lines or more, indent and write the passage *exactly as it appears in the text.* For example, suppose you were composing an interpretive paper on *Moby Dick.* Here's how you would quote a long passage:

Starbuck is haunted when he sees the great squid. There is a shocking revelation during this nightmarish encounter:

> As with a low sucking sound it slowly disappeared again, Starbuck still gazing at the agitated waters where it had sunk, with a wild voice exclaimed— "Almost rather had I seen Moby Dick and fought him, than to have seen thee, thou white ghost!"

B) **When eliminating part of a quote, use ellipses**. If you want to economize a long quote or establish fluidity, ellipses come in handy. Notice how ellipses are used to shorten the following quote:

The meteorologist said, "I would suggest packing your bags in anticipation of a mandatory evacuation, and then putting your belongings in your cars."

The meteorologist said, "I would suggest packing your bags...and then putting your belongings in your cars."

QUOTE INCORPORATION EXERCISES

(A) Copy five examples of quote incorporation in published writing. Newspapers, magazines and journals are good resources for this assignment. Keep in mind that we're not talking about dialogue here. We want examples of writers using direct quotes.

Beneath each example, explain the strategy the writer used. Can you offer any insight into the writer's choice of quote incorporation? Are there ellipses used? Is the quote divided? If so, why?

(B) Now it's your turn. Using **five** different strategies, incorporate the opening line of Willa Cather's *O Pioneers!* into an original sentence. Feel free to use only part of the sentence, and to use ellipses when necessary. One example is provided.

> "One January day, thirty years ago, the little town of Hanover, anchored on a windy Nebraska tableland, was trying not to be blown away."
>
> 1. When Willa Cather opens *O Pioneers!* she says, "One January day...the little town of Hanover, anchored on a windy Nebraska tableland, was trying not to be blown away."

Sentence Combining

Introduction to Composition Skills

This section of the book is devoted to exercising and improving your composition skills. This will be done primarily through sentence combining and revision practice. If you take these exercises seriously, they will help you develop into a more sophisticated, fluid, and expressive writer. Right now, "relative pronouns" and "participial phrases" probably sound intimidating, but the truth is that many of you already use these elements in your writing.

Beginning writers often have the tendency to compose their sentences in a predictable subject-verb sequence. The sentences are about the same length, becoming monotonous.

> This summer we visited Mexico. We flew from Miami to Mexico City. Then we took a cab to our hotel. We visited the Pyramids, and had some wonderful food.

Notice the repetition of the pronoun *we*, and the rather sing-songy tempo of the sentences. Here's a quick alternative:

> This summer we visited Mexico. We flew from Miami to Mexico city, took a cab to our hotel, visited the Pyramids, and had some wonderful food.

See the difference? The second sentence makes the description flow. Sometimes, of course, you want to repeat sentence structures, *but you want it to be your choice, not your habit.*

So, we'll begin practicing different structures through sentence combining exercises. Why? Because variety adds depth to your work. Writer Joan Didion says it best:

> All I know about grammar is its infinite power. To shift the structure of a sentence alters the meaning of that sentence, as definitely and inflexibly as the position of a camera alters the meaning of the object photographed. Many people know about camera angles, but not so many know about sentences.
>
> —Joan Didion, "Why I Write"

Once you complete these exercises, your writing should become smoother, and your sentences more complex. You will discover that the structure of a sentence actually helps determine its meaning. Finally, as you read a variety of literature, you'll be more aware of the writers' choices.

Sentence Combining Basics

We'll begin with some simple sentence combining exercises. Look at these sentences:

-The notice is on the bulletin board. The notice is important. It contains the schedule changes.

The subject, "the notice," opens each sentence, appearing as the pronoun "it" in the third sentence. Here's a sentence combining solution:

-The important notice about the schedule changes is on the bulletin board.

When revising, writers look for opportunities like these to combine sentences so that their work flows better, and so that subjects, pronouns and adjectives aren't repeated. They strive to achieve **economy of expression**. The more you look for opportunities, the more they will appear.

To bring our point home, study a piece of your recent writing. Do the sentences mirror one another? Are they similar in length? Is the subject in the same position?

SENTENCE COMBINING EXERCISES

We'll be using the following approach throughout our exercises, so please read these instructions carefully.

You are being asked to combine each sentence cluster, or group, into one sentence. Some of the clusters contain as few as two sentences, some contain four or more. For this first assignment, use any sentence combining strategy that feels comfortable, as long as the sentences are clear and grammatically sound. You are free to add and eliminate words, but don't change the meaning of the sentences. Later on, you'll practice specific strategies. Keep in mind that two good sentences are always better than one long muddled one! So, if you can't combine the whole cluster, don't force it.

Some of the sections are thematic, while others aren't. As you'll see, the clusters become increasingly challenging as you move along.

Note: When you're done with each section, you can compare your answers to those in the **Answer Key**, which begins on page 99. Remember that there is often a variety of correct responses. If you're not sure whether yours is correct, ask a teacher for help.

(A)

1. The pizza is on the table.
2. ~~The table is~~ in the living room.

3. India is an ancient country.
4. There are many dialects spoken in India, an ancient country

5. The ants are thirsty.
6. They are coming into our kitchen. The ants coming into our kitchen, in a single file line, are thirsty.
7. They are in a single file line.

8. Computers are very useful.
9. You can keep records on them. useful computers can keep records and can use the internet.
10. You can use the Internet, too.

(B)

1. Jerusalem is a sacred city.
2. ~~Jerusalem is~~ in Israel.

3. There are Jewish, ~~holy places.~~
4. ~~There are~~ Christian ~~holy places.~~
5. ~~There are~~ and Muslim holy places.

6. Many religious seekers travel to Jerusalem. Many religious seekers from all over the world, travel to the synagogues, churches, and mosques in Jerusalem.
7. They travel from all over the world.
8. They travel to synagogues, churches and mosques.

9. ~~Many civilizations~~ have occupied Jerusalem.
10. ~~These~~ civilizations including Babylonian, Roman, and Ottoman, have occupied Jerusalem

11. The most sacred Jewish site is the Western Wall,
12. T~~he Wall was~~ a piece of King Solomon's Temple,
13. T~~he Temple was~~ destroyed by the Romans in A.D. 70.

14. There are many Christian sites in and around Jerusalem,
15. The Way of Sorrows ~~is there~~.
16. ~~This is~~ believed to be the route Jesus walked before the Crucifixion, etc.

17. The central Muslim site, ~~is the Dome of the Rock~~. (1)
18. ~~It is~~ (1) a beautiful, colorful mosque, (2)
19. ~~It is~~ (2) believed to stand on the spot where Mohammed made his mystical flight to heaven, is the Dome of the Rock.

Relative Clauses

We continue our study of sentence construction with a review of relative clauses. Look carefully at the following sentence combining example. The relative is underlined; the relative clause is italicized.

-The cave is a mysterious place. The cave was discovered by some Boy Scouts.
-The cave, *which was discovered by Boy Scouts,* is a mysterious place.

Notice how the clause eliminates an entire sentence. The key word is "which". In this case, *which* is a **relative**. Do you see how it works to add information to the noun, "cave"? That's how relatives function: They modify nouns by adding details, eliminating needless repetition and creating a new structure called a **relative clause**. The placement of relative clauses also affects the emphasis of a sentence. For example, we could have constructed our sentence like this:

-The cave, *which is a mysterious place,* was discovered by Boy Scouts.

This version places more emphasis on the fact that the Scouts discovered the cave, doesn't it? It's important that you're aware of the shifts in meaning when you use relatives. We will look into this later.

Relatives include *which, who, whom, that* and *whose.* The relative you employ depends on the type of noun it replaces. *Who* and *whom,* for example, replace nouns that refer to people:

-Debbie, *who loves to garden,* planted the garlic yesterday.
-I gave the check to my landlady, *whom I have known for many years.*

The relative *who* tells us more about "Debbie," while *whom* adds information about the landlady. *Whose* replaces nouns that indicate ownership, or possessive nouns:

-Nothing can stop the superhero, *whose goal is to save the planet.*

Note: Be careful not to use *who's* for *whose. Who's* means "who is."

Some relatives are flexible and interchangeable. *That* can be used to modify people, animals or things. It can often be replaced by *which* or *who.* Notice, however, that *which* has a formal quality that appears a bit stilted:

-The mouse *that crawled under the refrigerator* made my mom unhappy.
-The mouse *which crawled under the refrigerator* made my mom unhappy.

In this next example, *that* is more emphatic, though either choice is correct:

-The girl *that won the race* is from New Zealand.
-The girl *who won the race* is from New Zealand.

Keep in mind that the meaning of a sentence might change with a relative clause, depending on your use of commas:

-Teenagers *who like to drive fast* are not using good judgment.
-Teenagers, *who like to drive fast*, are not using good judgment.

Do you see the difference? The first example means that *only* teenagers who drive fast are irresponsible; the next sentence implies that *all* teenagers drive fast, doesn't it? So, in this case commas are not needed!

On the other hand, commas are always needed when you're replacing a proper noun with a relative. Without commas, the sentences would be confusing and long-winded.

-Joey Crowell, *who lives in the new house down the street*, works for the city.
-My friend Jody, *whose talents include kite flying*, is taking the day off.

Stay sensitive to the punctuation requirements involved in relative clauses. In many cases the relative is optional:

-The waves, *which are full of unpredictable power*, are dangerous.
-The waves, *full of unpredictable power*, are dangerous.

Both examples are fine; it's a writer's choice, a matter of style. The next time you read an essay, be aware of relative clauses . Ask yourself how and why they're being used. In time, they should start surfacing in your writing. One warning: Don't overdo it! When we learn a new strategy, we tend to overuse it. Look at this passage:

> The stock market, which continues to rise and fall, is down again today. The stockbrokers, who are professionals who study the market, are sweating it out. My friend, whose money is invested in foreign stocks, is ignoring the economic happenings, which he claims are inconsequential in the long run.

While the relative clauses are used correctly, there are too many. It creates a predictable, monotonous sequence. Another word of caution: Be sure that the placement of the relative clause makes sense. Look at this sentence:

-The cry was the peacock's, which is living in our yard and sharing cat food.

Here, the possessive noun, "peacock's," cannot be modified by "which." A simple alternative would be as follows:

-The cry was from the peacock that is living in our yard.

RELATIVE CLAUSES EXERCISES

Using relative clauses, combine each of the following clusters into one sentence. Sometimes you'll have to shift the order of the sentences. You may add and eliminate words, but don't change the meaning. Underline the relative clauses. Here's an example:

1. The grapes are ripening on the vines.
2. The grapes will be used to make wine.
3. The wine will be expensive.

-The grapes, <u>which are ripening on the vines</u>, will be used to make expensive wine.

(A)

1. I might fill in for Mark.
2. Mark is going on a trip to Europe.

3. The pillow is very soft and comfortable.
4. The pillow is the largest in our house.

5. The history of Queen Elizabeth of England is chronicled in many books.
6. She signed the death warrant of Mary Queen of Scots.
7. She saw the Spanish Armada defeated.

8. Herman Melville wrote *Moby Dick* in 1851.
9. He is known for his stories of adventure on the sea.

10. Isaac's lollipop was missing.
11. It was found in the sofa.
12. It was sticking to the cushion.

(B)

1. The tourists gathered at the shore.
2. The tourists came from all over the nation.
3. They gathered to watch the speed boats.
4. The boats were slim and sleek.

5. The boats raced in twos.
6. They made a full circle around some buoys.
7. The buoys were more than a mile apart.

8. My dad's favorite boat was called *Jackknife*.
9. He cheered like a madman.

10. *Jackknife* failed when its engine caught fire.
11. *Jackknife* was leading the race.
12. The driver jumped overboard.

(C)

1. We took a train trip across the United States.
2. The trip was about 3,000 miles long.

3. The first part was through the California desert.
4. My friends slept through it.
5. They were tired.
6. I found the desert beautiful.

7. We played cards when we passed through the Great Plains.
8. I found the landscape boring.

9. By the time we reached the East Coast, Sheila was very unhappy.
10. Sheila's backpack was missing.

11. "I must have left it in St. Louis," she said.
12. "St. Louis is the last place I remember seeing it."
13. "It was at the depot."
14. "The depot was crowded."

(D) Now it's your turn. Using at least five relative clauses, write a one page piece describing the first fifteen minutes of your day. Underline the relative clauses once and the relatives twice.

(E) Copy five sentences from a published essay that employ relative clauses. Enter these and the title of the essay in your reading journal.

Participial Phrases

Now that you're familiar with relative clauses, let's move on to participial phrases. Study the following sentences. The participle is underlined; the participial phrase is italicized.

-*Moving along slowly*, the turtle finally reached the shore.
-The child, *weeping loudly*, was calmed by her mother.
-The skydiver, *falling through the air*, looked like a bodysurfer.

Can you see what these participles and phrases have in common? Look closely and you'll notice that a participle is **a verb that functions as an adjective**. A participial phrase contains a participle and its modifiers. In the first example, the participial phrase, "moving along slowly," modifies "turtle." The participle, "moving," acts as an adjective. In the second sentence, the participle "weeping" modifies "child." Can you see how the third example works? The verb, *fall*, becomes a participle when it describes the skydiver as "falling through the air."

We use participles all the time. They add variety and richness to our sentences. Can you identify the participial phrases below?

-Running without a helmet, the football player risked serious injury.
-Blessed with intelligence and wit, she is a great comic actress.

Got it? The phrases in these examples are "running without a helmet," and "Blessed with intelligence and wit." *Blessed* is a **past participle**. Past participles end in **-ed**. They are a more difficult to identify than the **present participle**, which ends in **-ing**.

Now let's see how participles can be used to combine sentences:

-The cartoonist drew the new character.
-He was laughing to himself.

-Laughing to himself, the cartoonist drew the new character.

"Laughing to himself" is a participial phrase modifying the cartoonist. It also emphasizes the laughter, doesn't it? So, by combining, you eliminate a sentence, you drop the repeated subject ("he"), and you add nuance to the meaning. And like relative clauses, participial phrases can be arranged in different parts of a sentence, depending on what kind of rhythm or emphasis you want. Here, "laughing to himself" is not as vital as it was in the previous version:

-The cartoonist, laughing to himself, drew the character.

When you start using participles, be careful where you place them:

-Gracing them with her lovely voice, the crowd was pleased.
-Having studied all day, what a great idea it was to see a movie.

See the problems? In the first sentence, the participial phrase creates a misplaced modifier. In the second, it causes a dangling modifier. (For a review, see page 23.) In both cases, your best bet is to place the noun as near to participial phrase as possible:

-Gracing them with her lovely voice, the singer pleased the crowd.
-Having studied all day, we thought a movie was a great idea.

PARTICIPIAL PHRASES EXERCISES

(A) Let's start by identifying participles and participial phrases. In each of the following sentences, underline the participial phrase.

1. Walking down the street, she noticed the overcast sky.

2. Blushing, the bride walked down the aisle.

3. Since we were mandated by the government, we bought a pass to go hiking.

4. Whispering a political speech, the five-year-old amazed the onlookers.

5. Mr. Pilwinker, attempting to inspire the students, gave an impassioned lecture.

6. I ran around to the back of the house when the lightning, striking with increased frequency, nearly hit me.

7. The flag, torn by the wind, was hanging like a rag.

8. The zebras walked out of the zoo unnoticed by the trainers.

9. Thrashing across the Atlantic, the hurricane hit North Carolina with ferocity.

10. The coffee, scalding my fingers, is too hot to drink.

(B) The next step is to put participles into practice through sentence combining. Using participles or participial phrases, combine each of the following clusters into one sentence. Underline the participle or participial phrase. Here is an example:

1. Polly is an annoying parrot.
2. Polly squawks Latin maxims all day long.

-<u>Squawking Latin maxims all day long</u>, Polly is an annoying parrot.

1. The team was excited about the bowling match.
2. They had been practicing all month.

3. The orange balloon was floating away.
4. It was followed by a sea gull.
5. The sea gull was curious.

6. The baby was riding in the car.
7. The baby fell asleep.

8. This evening I was bored.
9. I went stargazing and I saw Jupiter!

10. The customer was insistent.
11. The customer wanted to exchange 10,000 pennies for one hundred dollars.
12. She demanded to see the bank manager.

(C)

1. Paula brought the computer home.
2. She was very excited.
3. The computer was brand new.

4. Paula plugged in the computer.
5. As she did, she realized that she didn't know how to turn it on.

6. Paula was disappointed.
7. She read the instruction manual.

8. She thumbed through the pages.
9. She discovered that the instructions were in French.

10. Paula didn't bother to unplug the machine.
11. She jumped in her car and drove to the computer store.
12. She demanded that the manager give her a free tutorial!

(D) Now it's your turn to use participles. Using at least five participles or participial phrases, write a one page account of the last fifteen minutes of your day.

(E) Copy five sentences from a published essay that use participles or participial phrases. Enter these and the title of the essay in your reading journal.

Subordination

We have seen that the construction of a sentence helps determine its meaning. Sometimes these shades of meaning are subtle, sometimes they are dramatic. This is seen clearly when we use **subordination.** In life, a subordinate is someone who assumes an inferior rank, such as a private to a major, or an apprentice to a master. Similarly, in composition, subordination sets up a relationship between an independent and dependent clause. Grammatically speaking, one part is necessary (the independent clause), and the other is expendable (the dependent clause). Let's look at one example. The subordinate clause is underlined:

> -Although they had tried to save up for concert tickets, Fred and Martha ended up spending their money on yo-yos.

The independent clause is "Fred and Martha ended up spending their money on yo-yos." It's also the main idea of the sentence. The subordinate clause is dependent on more information and cannot stand on its own. However, it does determine the flavor of the sentence, suggesting that Fred and Martha tried but failed to save money. We will look into this more later. For now, let's study a list of common subordinates—words that initiate a dependent clause—along with the function they serve.

TO GIVE A REASON:	because, since, considering, given the fact that
TO SIGNIFY DEGREE:	to the degree that, to the extent that, inasmuch as
TO PROVIDE CONTRAST:	although, even though, though
TO SET UP A CONDITION:	if, assuming that, provided that, unless, whether or not, until
TO SIGNIFY TIME:	when, whenever, while, once, as long as, until
TO ESTABLISH PLACE:	where, wherever

Now let's see how subordination applies to sentence combining:

1. Stacy held the world record for continuous gum chewing.
2. Stacy's record was broken when Georgina, her sister, chewed a piece of Double Fruity for three weeks.

-Stacy held the world record for continuous gum chewing until her sister, Georgina, chewed a piece of Double Fruity for three weeks.

Notice how "until" allows you to combine sentences and to set up a cause and effect relationship. And as we said earlier, using subordination affects the sentence's meaning. It's up to you to decide which clause will be subordinate. Let's return to Fred and Martha:

-Although they had tried to save up for concert tickets, Fred and Martha ended up spending their money on yo-yos.

We don't know Fred and Martha, but this sentence emphasizes that they fell short of their goal to save money. Now look what happens when we reverse the clauses:

-Although Fred and Martha ended up spending their money on yo-yos, they had tried to save up for concert tickets.

Do you see how the emphasis in now on the fact that they had tried to save up? It makes us more sympathetic towards Fred and Martha, doesn't it? These are subtle but important differences!

Before you determine the sentence structure, you have to choose which subordinate best fits. Sometimes this will be evident; at other times it will be a writer's choice. Notice how different subordinate clauses are used to combine this pair of sentences:

1. We were pulled out by the rip tide and in danger of drowning.
2. The lifeguards rescued us.

-Because we were pulled out by the rip tide and in danger of drowning, the lifeguards rescued us.
-Before the lifeguards rescued us, we were pulled out by the rip tide and in danger of drowning.
-We were pulled out by the rip tide and in danger of drowning until the lifeguards rescued us.

Now, the general meaning of the sentence doesn't change, but the positioning of the three different subordinates determines the *sensibility* of the sentences. Study them for a moment. Can you see the differences?

Sometimes the choice and position of a subordinate can affect the meaning dramatically. Take the following examples:

-If you pass the physical, you will be allowed to join the team.
-Unless we clean the kitchen more thoroughly, the health inspector will close the restaurant down.

Because they are positioned at the opening of the sentence, these subordinate clauses have added emphasis. Also, the use of "if" and "unless" add a sense of urgency, suggesting that the physical might not be passed, and that the inspector just might close the restaurant down. Notice how the meanings change when we use different subordinates:

-When you pass the physical, you will be allowed to join the team.
-As long as we clean the kitchen more thoroughly, the health inspector will not close the restaurant down.

"When" and "As long as" create more optimism than exists in the previous versions, don't they?

To make matters more complex, the same subordinate can often appear in a variety of places, depending on the rhythm and sensibility you want to achieve. But again, you have to be careful. Here are three options for the same clause. Which one sounds awkward?

-Reading, if done daily, is helpful in building a strong vocabulary.
-If done daily, reading is helpful in building a strong vocabulary.
-Reading is helpful in building a strong vocabulary if done daily.

The first two examples are smooth, aren't they? But the third is difficult to read because the subordinate is so far removed from the subject, "reading."

SUBORDINATION EXERCISES

(A) Using twelve different subordinates (refer to the list on page 46), combine the two sentences below. Be sure that each function (time, degree, etc.) is represented **twice**. Remember that you're free to switch the order of the sentences. Underline the subordinate clause. One example is provided.

1. The pesticide levels are closely monitored.
2. The fruit is safe to eat.

-Assuming that the pesticide levels are closely monitored, the fruit is safe to eat.

(B) This is a three step exercise. First, using the identical subordinate clause, combine each of the following sentence groups into **two different sentences**. Next, discuss how the position of the subordinate clause affects the meaning of the sentences. Where is the emphasis? Is there added urgency? What about the rhythm? Did it make the sentence awkward? Is it grammatically sound? Finally, underline the subordinate clause. Here is an example:

1. I don't like the sight of needles.
2. I still donated blood.

-I still donated blood even though I don't like the sight of needles.
-Even though I don't like the sight of needles, I still donated blood.

—The second sentence emphasizes that the person doesn't like the sight of needles; it seems that he or she had more to overcome.

1. They boarded their windows against the storm.
2. The windows were smashed.

3. The gopher left its hole unoccupied for the day.
4. A snake slithered in and found a new home.

5. The cost of season tickets will increase.
6. The increase is estimated at 15%.
7. Fewer people will be able to afford to attend games.

8. I keep getting piles of junk mail every week.
9. I called the post office and complained.
10. The junk mail is useless.

11. George went on the bike ride.
12. George acted like Don Quixote.

(C) Now let's practice applying subordinates. Using at least five subordinate clauses, write a one page description of your favorite movie.

(D) Copy five sentences from a published essay that employ subordination. Enter these and the title of the essay in your reading journal.

Sentence Combining Finale

We will conclude our study of sentence construction by revising the following piece. Using relative pronouns, participles, and subordinates, rewrite the story. Look for sentence combining opportunities, but don't force them. The sentences should remain clear and varied.

Claire woke up. She rubbed her eyes. Then she smiled when she saw her beloved new puppy. It was asleep on the foot of her bed. The little cocker spaniel was named "Goldy." Claire pushed the blankets aside and cuddled up to Goldy. Claire's seventh birthday was celebrated the day before.

Claire heard a knock on her door. It was her father's knock. He always knocked four times. He told her to wake up and get dressed for school. Claire didn't want to go to school. She wanted to stay home with Goldy. The dog woke up and looked at Claire lovingly.

"I'm not feeling well, Daddy," said Claire. Then she manufactured a cough. "It's best if I stay home today," she said.

"What's wrong?" asked her father through the door.

"I seem to have developed a cough last night. I think the party was a little much for me," replied Claire.

"Okay," said her dad. He knew she wasn't really sick. "I guess that means I'll have to take Goldy for his walk today," he added.

Now Claire was trapped. She wanted to take her puppy to the park to play. Now she couldn't. Her father thought she was sick. She wrapped her arms around Goldy. She started to cry.

Claire's father could hear his daughter's quiet sobbing. He knew it was up to him to give her a way out. He remembered trying to skip school when he was a kid. He knocked on the door.

"You know," he said gently, "you might want to try to go to school. If you're still not feeling well, you can call us. Then we will go pick you up."

Claire's cheeks were streaked with tears. Claire gathered herself. "Okay, Dad, I'll give it a try," she said.

Four Essays

Introduction to Essay Writing

In this final section you are asked to apply what you've learned by writing essays. Before beginning, take a minute to familiarize yourself with the structure of the section.

You are assigned four different types of essays: (1) taking a stand, (2) compare and contrast, (3) personal, and (4) mock essay. The nature and demands of each of these is explained in detail. There are no time limits to the assignments. You are, however, encouraged to complete all of the essays, for each requires different reasoning and writing skills. There are many other kinds of essays, but these serve as good introductions.

Studying each section carefully will help prepare you for the particular demands of each paper. They include tips that will save you time, along with helpful examples. Each section contains the following parts:

- Reading Warm-up: You are asked to read published essays, studying them for the qualities highlighted in the section. This will help you see how the "pros" do it, while developing critical thinking skills. It is recommended that you respond to these essays in your reading journal.

- Writing Warm-up: These assignments are designed to jump-start the writing process, and to assist you in developing material for each essay.

- Student Essay: Each section culminates with a student essay. The essays are meant both for inspiration and for study. *Students and teachers should study these pieces carefully.*

When appropriate, **activities** and **group learning** opportunities are provided. The activities embrace the spirit of the essay, though they don't require writing. Group learning, as it suggests, provides opportunities for student interaction.

PEER EDITING

One final note: It's highly recommended that you read and respond to some of your peers' papers. While it may be awkward at first, it's best to read critically, providing comments that will help the writer along. By reading attentively and sensitively, with a constructive spirit, you will provide useful feedback. Furthermore, this process will develop your ability to read your own work objectively—not an easy task!

Taking a Stand:
The Art of the Argument

Suppose you live in the small town of Smithville, where the recreation department and a local developer have proposed building a new water park. You are strongly opposed to the project and you want to convince your city council members not to build the park. How are you going to go about convincing them? What makes a good argument? You can gather signatures, take out an ad in the local paper, or even picket city hall. These strategies might be helpful. Perhaps most effective, however, will be your use of words along with a competent argument. As you'll see, it's the order of your ideas, the balance of your appeal and the substance of your support that has the power to persuade people.

Given all the controversial issues, disparate beliefs, and vested interests out there, it's in your best interest to understand how a good argument works. Not only will you be able to formulate and compose one yourself, but you'll learn to see through a weak argument and protect yourself from manipulation. After all, words and ideas are very powerful tools. If you've ever read a good editorial or heard a riveting speech, you've witnessed the art of the argument. If you feel passionately about an issue, the skills you learn here will help you express your ideas convincingly. Finally, the prompts for college entrance exams usually ask you to take a side of an argument; the strategies you learn here will be useful.

ASSIGNMENT

Take a side on an issue you care deeply about. After assembling evidence, write a three-to-five-page double-spaced persuasive essay.

Your goal here is twofold: (1) you want to state your opinion clearly, and (2) you want to convince your reader to agree with your stand. Of course, when it comes to certain controversial issues, it will be impossible to shake some readers from their convictions. That's not important. For our purposes, assume you are writing to a neutral reader, someone who has not taken a side on the issue.

FINDING A TOPIC

For some, finding a topic won't be difficult at all; you might already know what you want to write about. If you have trouble deciding on an issue, look for ideas in the editorial section of your local or national newspaper. The editorial cartoons, along with the articles, will provide food for thought.

Your topic may or may not be of global importance. In fact, given the suggested length of your essay, a local issue might be more appropriate. Whatever your choice, it's important that you **limit yourself to a narrow topic**. Let's say you're interested in environmental issues. "The environment" is your topic. Okay, but it's likely that the range and complexity of this topic will lead to a lot of generalities; and as we have emphasized, being illustrative is the key to successful writing. Will you write about air pollution, water pollution, ozone depletion? How could you possibly attend to the complexity of the issue? What about narrowing it to "land development"? Getting there, but it's still pretty broad for a three to five page paper. Are there any local issues that involve land development? Let's return to our previous example: the proposed water park. Your new topic reads, "We should not build a water park in our town." Better, isn't it? This issue is narrow enough to drive the paper forward with a lot of momentum. It also invites field research, which we'll cover below.

Once you decide on an issue, *state it succinctly in the form of a stand that you're taking*. This will be your **thesis**, the fuel which propels the paper. For example, let's say your thesis is "the water park." This sounds like the title of a brochure from your local recreation department, doesn't it? Does this give the paper energy? Are we clear what the stand is? What about, "Should we have a water park?" Closer, but this is stated as a question, and you're not answering a question here—you're communicating a strong opinion *all the way through.* "We should not build a water park in our town" is an assertive, specific, and energetic thesis.

Topic exercise

Before continuing, let's take a look at some topics that are too general for our persuasive paper. For each of these, write down a specific alternative that would work, then formulate an assertive thesis narrow enough for our assignment. The first example is done for you.

Topic: Space travel.
Alternate: Space travel should be halted.
Thesis: Until we can solve our problems here on Earth, spending money on space travel is a horrible waste of taxpayers' money.

- censorship
- taxes
- immigration
- home schooling
- pollution
- gun control
- school uniforms
- endangered species

Developing your topic

First, take time to brainstorm about your topic. You can do this by yourself or in a group. Write down all the reasons why there shouldn't be a water park. Gather all the images that rise in your mind: Maybe there's a beautiful oak tree that will be destroyed if the park is built. This image might be useful in your paper. The key here is to write with abandon, to use free association to generate ideas and connections between ideas, to get it out without interference. (See page 16 if you need to review brainstorming.)

Gathering your evidence

You will need a certain amount of supporting points to get your argument across. After all, it's the facts behind your opinion that will help convince your readers. If you were writing a ten page research paper, you would need lots of citable sources. For our purposes, you can settle for a list of concrete reasons why your position makes sense. The richer your support, the better.

Before beginning, let's take a brief look at two approaches to research that will ensure a balance in your argument. If your case against the water park relied only on numbers and statistics, it might tire the reader; yet if it relied only on interviews and quotes, leaving out hard evidence, it probably won't convince an objective thinker. You want a balance of both, which leads us to the distinction between **library** and **field** research.

You've probably already experienced **library research,** which involves finding evidence in books, magazines, newspapers, and so forth. Your local librarian will be happy to help you locate sources. And now, with the Internet so accessible, you can "surf" the Web for material.

As you gather evidence, remember that it's always best to *find a variety of print sources.* Too often students limit themselves to one article, book, or website, narrowing their perspectives on issues and creating repetition in their papers. By citing at least a few different sources, you strengthen the scope of your argument.

Another creative and often overlooked approach is to use older material as evidence. It invites comparison and offers historical perspective. Suppose, for example, that you studied a history of your town and discovered that overdevelopment was already a concern thirty years ago. Wouldn't that enrich your argument? Wouldn't this be a good opening to your paper?

> Thirty years ago, Mayor John Smith stood on the corner of Main and 23rd, proposed site of the new water park, and expressed his concern: "It is essential, for both economic and aesthetic reasons, that we limit land development." "If we continue to build movie theaters and office buildings," he continued prophetically, "we will compromise our quality of life and the very flavor of Smithville."

This would be powerful, wouldn't it? It's illustrative, surprising, and proves to the reader that you've done your homework. By finding older sources, you can also juxtapose points of view that might have changed over time. For instance, 100 years ago land development was not the issue it is today. In fact, it's likely that very few people thought in terms of conservation at all. Couldn't you connect earlier attitudes to the lack of open space in your town, and ultimately to the water park?

> In the early part of the century, settlers to our valley looked upon a limitless expanse of land and possibility. Now it's a different story. First came Main Street, then the General Store, then the school, movie theater, bowling alley, and most recently the large housing developments. If we are to maintain our identity, if we are to share in the vision of our ancestors, we must put an end to development, beginning with the water park.

This dramatic introduction travels across time to convince the reader that the water park is a bad idea. As we have emphasized many times before, essay writing is a creative act! By using a variety of sources in your library research, you'll be able to make more of these creative connections. Now let's move on to field research.

Field research is a perfect complement to library research. It involves going out into the world and gathering evidence. Because you get to interact with people and visit places, field research can be a lot of fun—a bit like detective work. If you were a geologist writing a report on ruins, for example, your field research would involve digging and labeling. For our water park purposes, why not attend city council meetings or write letters to government officials? These would bring you up to date on the issue. In addition, consider using interviews and surveys to gather evidence. Let's take a minute to cover these strategies.

(a) **Interviews** are an exciting and valuable source of field research. Why not schedule an appointment to interview a county water official? You'll be surprised how most people will be more than happy to help. When choosing your subjects, be sure to interview someone opposed to your stand as well—in this case, someone in favor of a water park.

Prepare for the interview by writing down a list of questions. Bring a tape recorder along, and ask your subject for permission to use direct quotes from the interview. Once you're done, edit down the interview and use the quotes *sparingly* in your paper. While it's sometimes appropriate, it's unlikely that in a brief paper you'll want to write down a question and answer format.

Also, don't limit yourself to interviewing the authorities. Why not ask a seven year old about her thoughts on the water park? Traffic control is probably not high on her list of concerns, but her parents might think otherwise! Again, used appropriately, interviews will help balance and enrich your paper.

(b) **Surveys:** Making up a questionnaire about the water park. Not only will this inform you how the public feels, but if your questions are focused enough you're likely to find out what kind of person favors or opposes the park. It's best to leave the survey anonymous—that way people will be sure to answer honestly. Of course, you can simply have a "for or against" list, though your discoveries here will be limited. Here's a sample survey that would be useful for our topic:

```
Age:
Sex:
Occupation:
Marital Status:
Number of family members:
How long have you lived in Smithville?
What is your annual income?
What are your hobbies?
What school, if any, do you attend?
Are you in favor of the water park? Why
  or why not?
```

Once you gather enough questionnaires, see whether there's a connection between how long someone has lived in town and his opinion on the water park. Perhaps you'll find that people with higher incomes prefer not to have the park built. What would that suggest? As you can see, surveys provide insight into the issue.

Statistics, whether garnered from library or field research, are indispensable to most arguments. However, don't be surprised if you find that even "official" statistics contradict each other, for the outcome of statistical research is sometimes defined by the vested interests involved in gathering them. (The interpretation of statistics makes matters even more complex.) If you've ever heard political debates, you know that statistics are subjective. In your case, you want to find confirmed statistics and use them for support. Remember, though, they're malleable! That's why it's up to you to have your intelligence bear on them. Suppose, for example, that the water park will receive an estimated 750 visitors per week. Here are two interpretations of this statistic:

> According to environmental impact reports, it is estimated that the water park will receive about 750 visitors weekly. Can you imagine those crowds bursting through Main Street every week? Think about the impact on traffic, noise and air pollution—not to mention crime! We simply can't absorb this many people and keep our sanity.

According to environmental impact reports, it is estimated that the water park will receive about 750 visitors weekly. This might seem like a lot of people, but remember that the vast majority will arrive on weekends, keeping our streets quiet during the week. Also, these numbers are based on a yearly projection—during the colder winter months there will be fewer visitors. So don't let that number scare you. The added revenue and excitement outweighs the exaggerated impact.

Got the point? Same statistic—opposite interpretations!

Note: Be sure to credit your sources throughout your paper. Unless you're turning this into a research paper, you don't need footnotes. However, any hard evidence or direct quotes should be cited, typically by placing the name of the source before the material. For example,

According to Sally Jones, editor of "The Smithville Reporter," there have been far more letters of complaint against the water park than letters in favor of it.

This establishes the source of the information, giving you credibility. Now if someone doubts you, they can follow through with Sally Jones. One rule to remember: If you think someone might doubt your information, establish your source. With general knowledge, however, you don't always need a source. "California is the second largest state," doesn't need to be cited.

Attend to the opposing viewpoints. This is an essential step in putting together a solid argument. In a political debate candidates spend lots of time predicting their opponents' arguments. They know what to expect and they are ready to respond. The same logic applies to a persuasive essay. The important step for us, then, is to make a list of arguments *in favor* of the water park:

1. Raise money.
2. Create jobs.
3. Lots of fun for the kids.
4. A place for families that don't have a swimming pool.
5. Attract tourists.
6. A safe place for teenagers to hang out instead of hanging around town with nothing to do.
7. We already have a lot of open space, so developing a few more acres won't make that much of a difference.
8. If it doesn't work, we can take it down!

This is a perfect opportunity to work in groups. Take turns explaining your position and have other group members act as the opposition, throwing out all the objections they can think of. Once you list these objections, don't be surprised if your position is swayed in some way. You might have to start over or redefine your stand. While this would be frustrating, you will have saved a great deal of time in the long run.

If you're ready to proceed, then you need to attend to these opposing arguments. The thoughtful reader (not to mention the one opposed to your stand) will consider them, so it's up to you to disclaim them. Not only will this make your argument more sound, but it may provide structure for your paper. Notice how these paragraphs feed off opposing arguments:

> Proponents of the water park say it will raise money. Don't be so sure. What about property tax, insurance, and maintenance? What if an amusement park is built in a neighboring county and we lose 30% of our visitors?
>
> Yes, jobs will be created, but how many and for how long? Once the construction is done, how many employees will it take to run the show? Some custodians, a couple of lifeguards, a few snack bar people....
>
> The argument that we have lots of open space surrounding Smithville is absurd. The truth is that open space within town limits is disappearing fast. And to suggest that we can simply remove the park if it doesn't succeed is nuts, for the land would already be destroyed.

As you see, all three paragraphs highlight opposing points as a kind of counterbalance for argument. They employ evidence effectively, and invite an assertive tone.

WRITING YOUR PAPER

What follows is a list of important guidelines to keep in mind as you write your paper. Study this list carefully. Following these suggestions will ensure that you're approaching the essay properly. Once you complete your first draft, revisit this list.

(1) **Take your stand assertively.** Because most issues are sensitive and complex, students often feel compelled to qualify their stand throughout their paper. This can result in a wishy-washy tone that will defeat the purpose of the paper:

> It seems to me that the water park would cause problems in the community. I know the slides would be a lot of fun, but there will be so many cars coming through town, I'm just not sure it's worth it.

Get the idea? Qualifiers like "it seems to me," and "I'm just not sure," drain the energy from the paper. On the other hand, you don't want to confront your reader too aggressively either. No one likes a lecture, and you run the risk of coming across as righteous:

> `Any Smithville resident who thinks the water park is a good idea should move away. Who wants more visitors? Who wants more noise? And for what? A bit of revenue? Proponents of the water park are obviously shortsighted and don't truly care about the quality of life in Smithville.`

Even a neutral reader would likely be offended by this tone. What's worse, this confrontation might sway the reader to the opposite side of the argument—an unfortunate irony!

(2) **You're job is to take a stand, not to provide a solution to a problem.** Keep your writing focused on your stand. While there might be some room to discuss a solution, it should be minimal and should not take away from the focus. It's very easy to get sidetracked and lose your audience. Don't spend too much time suggesting that a wildlife organization might be able to buy up the water park land, for example. Leave solutions to another paper.

(3) **Establish common ground.** If you're hoping to genuinely reach your audience, establishing common ground is vital. You want the reader to feel like you're looking at the issue together, and that you share her concerns, that you're a sensible person—even if you feel differently:

> `We all want a peaceful town. We all want a prosperous town with good schools for our children. While the water park might bring us some revenue and create a few jobs, the cost to our way of life would be greater than the money we bring in.`

The writer establishes a tone of shared concern while remaining assertive—a nice combination. The common ground gets the reader involved in the paper. This leads us to the fourth guideline.

(4) **Balance your argument by appealing to your reader's reason and emotion.** As we have said, a good argument is a balanced argument. If you rely primarily on emotions, you might come across as blubbery and manipulative. But if you pack your paper with statistics without appealing to feelings, you might lose half your audience. You also want to appeal to your reader's **ethical** side. If you convince your reader why opposing the water park is in fact an ethical, or moral choice, you've gained a lot of ground:

```
     All over the country small towns like Smithville are
caving in to the spread of commercialism and entertainment,
going for the short-term gain at the expense of the future.
While it might be difficult to reject the water park, by
doing so we will be securing a more peaceful atmosphere for
our children, and sending a message of hope to small towns
all over America.
```

This passage is appealing because it calls on the reader's depth of character without sounding preachy or condescending. Again, it's all a matter of balance.

READING WARM-UP

(A) Study the student essay on page 63, "Skateboarding is Not a Crime," by Mark Garcia. Share your impressions with classmates. What kind of evidence does Mark use? Is the argument convincing? Balanced? Is the writing clear? Enter your impressions in your reading journal.

(B) Taking a stand essays are as close as the editorial section of your local or national newspaper. An editorial is an article that expresses the opinion of an editor or contributing writer. Editorials might not be as developed as full length essays, but they are useful places to begin. Read several editorials. How are they structured? Do they use enough specifics? What about their tone? Are they appealing? Are they convincing? Why or why not?

(C) Now study a few persuasive essays from published collections. Again, consider all areas of the essay. Enter your thoughts in your reading journal.

WRITING WARM-UP

Listed below are several controversial statements. Choose a few and write a one page essay taking one side of the argument. While you won't be expected to write a comprehensive essay, this exercise will help develop your skills.

- Women should stay at home and care for their children.
- Immigration should be halted.
- Spanking is a good way to discipline children.
- Euthanasia should be against the law.
- The use of nuclear power should be increased.

ACTIVITIES

This activity is popular in speech and debate classes. It's called "**sparring**." All you need are two volunteers, an audience, and a debatable topic.

First, designate a leader. Then have everyone write down a topic on slips of paper. The leader chooses one of these topics at random—which she reveals to the volunteers only—and then designates which side of the debate each volunteer will represent. This is entertaining and valuable because you might be forced to argue for something you don't believe.

Next, give the volunteers a few minutes to prepare for their sparring debate. When they're ready, allow each a one minute opening statement arguing his case. Follow this with 30 second rebuttals, and then 30 second closing statements. Feel free to structure the timing differently.

When the debators are through, ask the audience who won the debate and why. While this exercise involves speaking skills, quick thinking, and performance ability, it also challenges you to create a specific argument while "sparring" against your opponent's ideas.

EXTENSION

(A) Write another taking a stand essay **opposing** your own essay. Despite the moral discomfort, this piece will help strengthen your writing and thinking skills, highlighting the objective features of a good argument.

(B) Using the strategies you've learned, write an editorial to a local or national paper.

Skateboarding is Not a Crime
by Mark Garcia

Today, when school was out, my friends and I rushed to our homes, grabbed our water bottles, hoped on our boards, and skated to the parking lot behind the bank. Doug, Amy, and I began practicing our jumps off the slanting concrete wall. Doug tweeked his ankle while flipping his board, but a few minutes later he was back at it. After weeks of practice, Amy perfected her triple 360's. I still haven't got it, but when I have the time between homework and chores, I keep at it. Suddenly our session was halted when a police car pulled into the parking lot. The officers warned us that we would be ticketed the next time we're found there.

This is what it's been like for years now. Though we have been campaigning for a skateboard park, for one reason or another the city will not build one. All around our small town of Mitton, kids like us are frustrated. And there are a lot of us! We can't skate on empty parking lots, or sidewalks, or even the streets. If they don't want us skating in town, then why not build us a skateboard park? One thing is for sure: We are not going away, we will not stop skating, and skateboarding is not a crime!

Some people argue that a skateboard park would attract lots of undesirable outsiders to Mitton. "The last thing we want," says Bob Townsend, a citizen of Mitton, "is a bunch of troublemaker skateboarders coming up here every day." Since both Parker and North Hills already have skateboard parks, it's doubtful kids will flock over here.

It's also evident that Mr. Townsend hasn't hung around many skateboarders. His statement shows just how stereotyped we have become. Yes, there are some troublemakers, but every group has them! Most of us just want a place to ride and to hone our skills. Maybe it's the baggy pants (in style for now), or the fact that we're teenagers that scares some people off. What most people don't see are the hours and hours of practice we put into perfecting our skills. We could be watching T.V. or hanging out in the mall, when instead we're outside getting exercise.

Like any other recreation facility, the skateboard park would have appropriate security. If a troublemaker came along, he or she would be kicked out. It's the same way in Parker, where they have very few incidents. According to the manager, Tammy McCarthy, most of the trouble is minor: "Once in a while a couple of skaters competing for the same ramp start yelling, stuff like that. But in the three years I've worked here, we've only had a few minor problems." This doesn't sound like a hotbed for anarchy, does it?

Ironically, those people concerned about safety should be in favor of a skateboard park. If we have a place to go, we won't be on the streets "tearing up" the concrete and getting in the way of cars. Since the park would be monitored, we would keep out of trouble while practicing the sport we love.

Another argument against the park involves money. City council members have argued that the park would cost too much to build, and that the town's tax payers wouldn't be willing to fund it. According to my research, this simply isn't true. I surveyed 100 taxpaying citizens in town, and 67% said they would accept a tax increase to help build a park. This goes to show that most people want a place for young people to hang out. They know that there's not much for us to do in Mitton. (Drinking decaf at Josey's Cafe is getting old.) Furthermore, in a few years the park would pay for itself, and even begin to bring revenue into the city, making it a worthwhile investment. This is what happened in Parker and in North Hills, and there's no reason to assume it wouldn't happen here.

The third major complaint against the park has to do with location: where to build it? No one wants the noise and crowds near his or her neighborhood. In a small town like ours, this is understandable. That's why it was recommended that the park be built behind the public parking lot in the heart of town. The land there is zoned for development, and there's more than enough acreage for a park. Some city council members rejected the idea, however, because they thought a skateboard park would be an eyesore to tourists. I'm no landscape designer, but can't we build an attractive boundary, put up a tall fence and plant some ivy, or paint a mural? The parking area for the skateboard park would be away from Main Street, limiting the direct traffic; and because the park will close at sundown, people who live near town can still sit down for quiet dinners.

As you can see, the skateboard park is not only a good idea for skateboarders, but for the community as well. I leave you with the words of Mark Green, owner of the park in North Hills:

> There was a lot of opposition when we first broke ground here. Someone even threatened to sue the city. But after a few months, we were no different than the health club down the street. It's just that the young people here ride their skateboards and the older types run on their treadmills.

Compare and Contrast: Building Meaning

What's a better place for an aspiring actor to live: California or New York? What are the similarities and differences between a Chevrolet and a Honda? What are the benefits and risks of investing in the stock market or real estate? These are examples of questions that would be answered in a compare and contrast essay.

Comparison highlights similarities, while contrast highlights differences. When you think about it, aren't you always comparing and contrasting possibilities: which shirt to wear? which computer to buy? what to have for breakfast? Maybe you're comparing and contrasting to prove a point: swimming is better exercise than running, or one candidate is more worthy than another.

Now it's your turn to pick two subjects to compare and contrast. It's best to choose a topic that really matters to you. Suppose you have to make a major decision soon. Looking carefully into the pros and cons of each possibility will help you make the right choice. As you'll see, there is practical value in writing an essay of this sort. Not only is comparing and contrasting a common technique in writing, but it exercises your ability to reason and to think abstractly, *to make connections and to build meaning*. This ability is helpful in all areas of study.

ASSIGNMENT

Write a three-to-five-page double-spaced essay comparing and contrasting two subjects.

Your primary goal is to highlight the similarities and differences between two subjects for a single purpose. This purpose will give your paper direction. We'll go into this in depth below.

FINDING A TOPIC

It's best if your topic has some relevance to your life. Maybe you're getting ready for college and want to compare two institutions to see which is better suited to your needs. Also, make sure that the subjects are different enough to contrast yet have something in common. You'll have a hard time comparing and contrasting rocks to pebbles, just as you would starfish to violins. That's not to say you can't be creative and push the limits. How about comparing astronauts to secretaries? Is there room for contrast? Certainly. Is there room for comparison? Probably, though you might have to stretch it!

It's important to choose a topic that will lend itself to lively details rather than sweeping generalizations. For example, "good weather and bad weather" is okay, but it runs the risk of being boring. What will your subtopics be? A sunny and a rainy day? How about comparing two violent weather phenomena, like hurricanes and tornadoes? There are enough dramatic details to make it interesting and to allow for discovery. Like any essay, it's the specifics that give the paper life and justify your purpose.

If you haven't already decided on a topic, go ahead and brainstorm possibilities. Are there two actors or movies you would like to parallel? Sports teams? Politicians? Countries? Summer and winter residences? Yourself and a sibling? Driving versus walking? The possibilities are endless—just don't choose something too ambitious, like North America and South America. This would require a book length project!

Defining your purpose

Once you decide on a pair of subjects, keep the comparison *succinct and purposeful.* Why are you juxtaposing these two things? Continuing with our colleges example, your topic might begin as "Mountain State versus Technical Institute." Okay, but what are you going to cover here? The history of each school? The alumni contributions? It's more focused if you say, "Mountain State and Technical Institute—which college should I attend?" This will give you an angle to pursue and a purpose for the comparison. Now your subtopics will relate to your position as an incoming freshman.

Keep in mind that your purpose doesn't have to involve choosing between things or taking a stand. It might simply celebrate the qualities of each subject. You could couple lake fishing and fly fishing. Your purpose? To define what each offers and to educate your reader.

Developing your topic

You can do this by yourself or in a group. Begin by listing the qualities of each of your subjects and then drawing connections between them. Use free association to generate ideas. The goal here is to actually discover connections.

Once you have your list, make two columns: one for similarities and one for differences. This would help move your paper towards a structure. Returning to our colleges, your columns might look something like this:

SIMILARITIES	DIFFERENCES
- w/in an hr. drive	- State has 25,000/Tech 8,000
- 4 year schools	- St.has a good sports program
- reputable	- Tech has cutting edge computer facilities
- good gen. ed programs	- Tech more geared for my career interests
- good dorm life	- St. students outdoorsy and sociable
- both diverse in own ways	- Tech students have clubs, but not out on the town much
- close to civilization and nature	- St. is in mountains
- good golf teams!	

Notice that these brief lists (you'll want to write more) don't include many generalities. Details guarantee an illustrative paper. "They're both nice places" is a fine sentiment, but it doesn't say much.

Once you've completed your list, decide on a few areas that you'll feature in your essay, areas that are relevant to your choice as an incoming freshman. Let's say you came up with (1) student body, (2) education, and (3) location. Now you're ready for the next important step: structuring your essay.

Structuring your essay

The structure of a compare and contrast paper is especially important. Without an effective outline to begin with, you could end up with an unfocused, unbalanced essay.

The most important step is to *balance your emphasis*. Too often, students spend the bulk of the paper highlighting one subject at the expense of the other. Either they favor one side, don't have enough information, or run out of room because they haven't outlined properly. Therefore, it's worth looking at a few approaches to structure particular to the compare and contrast essay.

One approach is to simply split the paper in half, dividing it into similarities and differences. You can also explore one subject at a time. In this case, the body of the outline might look like the one on the following page. **Note:** For our purposes, we will fill in details for the subtopics only once.

Thesis: While Mountain State offers some unique opportunities, after comparing it to Technical State, I feel that Tech is a better choice for me.

I. Mountain State
  A. Student Body
    1. Size
      a) 25,00 students
      b) growing!
    2. Diversity
      a) most students are from in-state
      b) very diverse racially
      c) economically diverse
    3. Student body
      a) a bit "laid back" and "outdoorsy"
      b) active part of the community
  B. Education
  C. Location

II. Tech College
  A. Student Body
    1. Size
      a) 8,000 students
      b) this is the school limit
    2. Diversity
      a) about half the students from in-state
      b) lots of international students
      c) mostly upper middle class
    3. Student body
      a) very serious students
      b) despite its location, students not very involved in community.
      c) lots of school spirit in the form of clubs and networks with other technical schools
  B. Education
  C. Location

This approach is straightforward and clear. However, it has some drawbacks. By focusing on one subject at a time, you risk losing the compare and contrast spirit of the paper. The points you made about Mountain State might be diluted once the reader gets to Tech College. For a paper of our size, though, it's a reasonable approach.

Another strategy is to alternate the colleges by placing the subtopics from above as the main topics. This approach keeps the subjects more closely related.

```
I. Student Body
     A. Mountain State
        1.Size
        2.Diversity
     B. Tech College
        1.Size
        2.Diversity

II. Education
     A. Mountain State
     B. Tech College

III. Location
     A. Mountain State
     B. Tech College
```

Get the idea here? Notice how the three sections include both colleges, allowing for a more immediate relationship than the first outline.

The third approach sets the schools side-by-side in each paragraph. This is a very inviting yet demanding approach. Because the comparisons and contrasts are so immediate, it takes sharp writing to pull it off.

```
I. Student Body
     A. Size
        1. State
        2. Tech
     B. Diversity
        1. State
        2. Tech
     C. General flavor and reputation
        1. State
        2. Tech

II. Educational

III. Location
```

In this approach, your subjects neighbor each other even more closely, sometimes within the same sentence: "State boasts a student body of 25,000, while Tech has a mere 8,000." How you distribute the details here is up to you; the key is that you're keeping the subjects together in the same paragraph.

WRITING YOUR PAPER

Here is a list of some do's and don'ts particular to the compare and contrast essay. Keep these suggestions in mind as you write your paper. Once you're done with your first draft, use this as a checklist.

(1) **Keep your purpose for comparing alive**. As mentioned earlier, it's the spirit of your inquiry into the two subjects that counts. Why are you comparing them? What kind of meaning will you be building? In our case, you're trying to discover which school is better for you. Transitions and conclusive phrases will help remind your reader what you're after. Look at this sample paragraph. Is the purpose for the paper clear?

> There's a disparity between the populations at Tech, which is limited to 8,000 students, and State, which has a 25,000 member student body. Even though State's campus is much larger, the thought of seeing tens of thousands of faces every week is a bit intimidating. And the population is growing! At Tech there will be more friendly faces.

Notice that the paragraph contrasts the figures for the purpose of seeing which population better suits the writer's tastes. The reasoning is clear and the writing smooth.

To ensure that your purpose remains alive, try this experiment: Write your thesis on a slip of paper, and set it in front of **every** paragraph in your essay. Does the paragraph relate to the thesis, at least indirectly? If not, ask yourself whether you've digressed, whether the information helps the thesis unfold.

(2) **Give each subject equal emphasis**. We covered this in terms of structure, but it bears repeating; for even if you have a balanced outline, it's easy to overemphasize one subject. This is especially likely to happen if you happen to favor one subject over another, or you haven't done the necessary research. Look at this paragraph:

> Mountain State has the reputation of being "outdoorsy" and "laid back." The friendly students would rather snowboard than attend lectures. But when it comes to sports, it's an energetic and spirited group. The football games, preceded by noisy pep rallies, are always sold out. Tech College, on the other hand, is known for its introverted "cyber" students. I guess there's not much going on there.

Tech gets the short end of the stick in this paragraph, doesn't it? The last sentence suggests that the writer didn't put much effort into finding out what activities take place there. What about school clubs and networking efforts?

Now, having a balanced emphasis doesn't mean that you can't have a strong opinion or an assertive tone. As long as you give equal attention, you can have any kind of tone or writing style that's appropriate. How you interpret the details is up to you—it's a creative act:

> Mountain State is populated by snowboarding, granola-eating students who like to hang out at coffee shops. But when there's a football game, they're prehistoric, full of ferocious school spirit. At Tech, students pass their time usefully by sitting in front of their PCs, downloading their websites, and programming new games. In the evenings the future cutting-edge entrepreneurs congregate civilly for their chess and movie clubs.

This is a highly stylized, biased paragraph in favor of Tech. It is, however, balanced, contrasting the schools methodically.

(3) **Keep your writing vivid**. While this piece of advice applies to all writing, it's especially relevant here. Because you'll be going back and forth between subjects, the paper runs the risk of becoming predictable and dull. When it begins to sound like a tennis rally that never ends, watch out! It's up to you to add liveliness and to give it breathing room. The sample paragraph above is a good example of lively writing. It moves back and forth purposefully, establishing a strong tone and using well chosen words. Unless you're attentive to these elements, you're liable to write a paper that sounds like this:

> At both Mountain and Tech, there are lots of students from in state. At Mountain, the student body is racially diverse; a lot of minority groups are represented. At Tech, there are lots of international students, but not a lot of minorities from the United States. The students who attend Mountain are from a variety of socioeconomic backgrounds, whereas at Tech most of the people are from upper middle class families.

Yes, it's clear, but it's boring. Can you imagine reading an entire essay that sounds like this? You're reader is likely to put the paper aside, fall asleep, or forget the important details. Here's an alternative that contains the same information:

```
Both Mountain and Tech have a lot of students from in
state, giving them a local feel. But at State you'll find a
diverse student body that represents lots of minority groups.
Don't be surprised to have a class include African, Mexican
and Native American students. At Tech, there's diversity, but
it's in the form of international students, many of them
Asian. Tech students tend to come from upper middle class
families, and to own their own cars and cutting-edge
computers. At State, students are more likely to cruise
around on their bikes and take the bus home.
```

The difference is obvious. This paragraph, while getting across the same information, brings both campuses to life through illustration, a conversational tone and skillful writing. You get a sense of the writer who is patching this information together.

READING WARM-UP

(A) Study the student essay on page 75, "Can That Rope," by James Usher. Share your impressions with classmates. What kind of comparing and contrasting strategies does James use? Is the purpose for the comparison clear? Is the writing good? Enter your impressions in your reading journal.

(B) Read a few published essays, looking for compare and contrast strategies. Enter your responses into your journal.

(C) Recreate the outline of a published essay. Identify each topic and subtopic and write a formal outline for the paper. This will give you some insight into the structure as well as the writer's choices.

WRITING WARM-UP

(A) Write a boring "back and forth" paragraph comparing and contrasting walking and riding a bike. Rewrite the paragraph so that it's inviting and smooth. Be sure that the rewrite contains the same information.

(B) Write a few one page essays comparing and contrasting some of the subjects below. Begin each essay by making a list of similarities and differences. The last two topics ask you to stretch your imagination a bit.

- Money and bartering as ways of exchanging goods
- Compulsory education and home schooling in terms of social development
- New York City and Boston as cities to visit
- The experience of flying on one airline versus another
- What you miss and gain by camping in a tent or a motor home

(continued)

- Snowboarding and skiing
- Animation from Japan and from the United States
- The Boy Scouts and the Girl Scouts
- Going for a checkup at the doctor and taking a test
- Sponges and people

GROUP LEARNING

Write a short essay comparing and contrasting yourself and a partner. Begin by focusing on one area of life: hobbies, family, career goals, or religious background, for example. Once you have decided, generate a list of compare and contrast details and then structure your paper accordingly.

When you're done, read the essay aloud to your classmates. This exercise helps build compare and contrast skills. It's also lots of fun.

ACTIVITIES

Comparing and contrasting techniques are common in advertising. How often have you seen an ad that reads something like, "Our detergent kills germs twice as fast as our leading competitor's," or "Test drive our newest model—it has the feel and austerity of a Rolls Royce for one-third the cost"?

Gather several television or print ads that use compare and contrast to appeal to the consumer. Write about them in your journal. Are they effective? How do they build meaning? Share your findings with your classmates.

EXTENSION

Compare and contrast essays lend themselves very nicely to visual representation. Wouldn't a collage of images from the Mountain State and Tech College catalogues be a fitting complement to the essay? It would employ the same strategies, only visually.

Can That Rope
by James Usher

It was not an unusual trip. The Boy Scout troop that I was guiding was experienced and competent—that is, until the day we got into camp a little late. The selection of trees on which to hang bear bags was not very good and the hour was late. In their rush to get to sleep the troop did a poor job hanging the bear bags. Waking the next morning, they were dismayed to find their food bags ripped to shreds and all of their food missing.

Bears are curious and intelligent, and always searching for food. The old school techniques of food storage are one of the many causes of conflicts between bears and humans. Exposure to human food can be a bear cub's death sentence, for it often leads to a "problem bear" in adulthood. Despite regulations and education, backpackers are still hesitant to shift from the old food storage techniques of bear bagging to the improved method of carrying a prefabricated canister for food storage.

The average adult black bear needs between 8,000 to 10,000 calories per day. Compare that to a human, who needs 2,500 daily calories. And as winter approaches, we pull sweaters from our closets to accommodate the chill, while a bear must increase its caloric intake to about 20,000 calories per day in order to store enough fat to sleep through the winter. A bear's general diet consists of natural foods such as berries, acorns, ants, and carrion. To get the appropriate number of calories a bear would need to eat these foods all day long; but if it follows a backpacker and steals her food, then the bear will come close to his caloric intake for the day. If you were the bear, which would you choose?

To avoid losing food to bears, campers have come up with a variety of techniques, some that work well and some that don't. The two most popular ways to store food include the counter-balance method and the bear canister. To counter-balance your food you need a tree branch about 15 feet off the ground (the branch also needs to measure 4 to 5 inches around at the base and taper down to about one inch at the end), a rope about an 1/8 of an inch in diameter, and two nylon bags to store your food and other smell-ables. A bear canister, on the other hand, is what it sounds like: a heavy-duty ABS plastic cylinder that measures 12 inches by 8 inches.

The cost of counter-balancing is relatively cheap. Fifty feet of 1/8 inch rope costs about $10, and the two nylon bags another $10. The going price for a bear canister is $78, and if you need the nylon carrying case, add another $17. With the price difference so great, wouldn't everybody be better off opting for the counter-balance method?

Not entirely. In Denali National Park most of the terrain is above the timberline. And even in the forested areas, the Park Service has required the use of bear canisters. According to park officials, since this requirement was implemented in 1984, there has been a 95 percent drop in cases of food loss to bears, along with an 85 percent drop in property damage.

During 1997 alone, bears caused $600,000 worth of property damage in Yosemite National Park, where bear canisters are not mandatory. And that was in the 5 percent of the park that is known as "front-country," or developed areas. What about the other 95 percent that is back country?

Counter-balancing is still allowed in the Yosemite back country, but that may be changing. The Yosemite wilderness is some of the most beautiful around, and home to some of the smartest bears. In some parts of the park, it is not uncommon to spend sleepless nights chasing away bears that come sniffing around for food. Sometimes, a sow will send her cub up into a tree, where the instinctive fellow jumps on the branch until it breaks, sending both cub and food flying to the ground. There have been reports of bears taking flying leaps off the trees, snagging the food bag on their way down. Conversely, there have been no reports of campers losing food from a bear canister. The canisters are too big for the bear to get his mouth around; they can't be crushed, and the lid has two flush mount screws holding it on. To the best of my knowledge bears haven't yet figured out how to use a Swiss army knife.

Which method is better? If you've ever spent 45 minutes looking for the perfect tree, another hour trying to throw the rope over the branch and hang the bags, and then a restless night worrying about the food bags, it is an easy choice. Or you can ask that Scout troop that I hiked in with. I spent a full day trying to get them to rent bear canisters, and their response was always the same: "We've never lost a bag to a bear yet." Unfortunately for them, they had a 20 mile hike out—without food. I was kind enough to share some of my snacks with them, the snacks that I pulled out from my bear canister.

The Personal Essay: An Act of Discovery

For you it might have been a game of hopscotch, a favorite teacher, a summer vacation home; it might have been falling in love, or a backpacking trip. Maybe it was something traumatic, or a tragedy: a car accident, a death in the family, a best friend moving away. We have all had formative, memorable experiences and relationships. It's these kinds of experiences that provide the substance of a personal essay.

While the two previous essays involved gathering information from the "outside world," the territory here is the writer's memories. Instead of facts and statistics, the personal essay is supported by the details of the writer's life; the "research" might involve some conversations with family members or visits to special places.

A good personal essay is like a good movie—it allows the reader to feel the texture of the writer's memories, to feel like she's there. So whether you're remembering a person, place, or event, your particular challenge here is to bring it to life for yourself and for the reader.

Writing this essay offers many personal rewards. For instance, there is the opportunity to come to terms with a difficult passage of life, or to celebrate a happy one. By writing about an experience with patience and care, you will be able to translate its significance and, hopefully, discover something for yourself. This is challenging but very worthwhile.

In addition to this personal value, writing the essay exercises your ability to remember and order memories in a meaningful way—an essential skill in both essay and imaginative writing. Finally, there's the challenge of maintaining an intimate feel for the reader—it's quite a balancing act.

ASSIGNMENT

Write a three-to-five-page double-spaced personal essay.

Your goal here is twofold: (1) to explore and recreate a meaningful experience in your life, and (2) to bring the reader along with you in an act of discovery. We will go into this in depth below.

FINDING A TOPIC

Finding a topic for a personal essay might be hard—not for a shortage of material, but because there's so much of it! Once you start brainstorming, once you open the treasure house of childhood, you'll find many opportunities for exploration.

What kinds of experiences are suitable for a personal essay? Anything—as long as you are able to communicate it to the reader. It would be helpful, however, to think about it in terms of three possibilities: (1) a person, (2) a place, or (3) an event. These will overlap, but finding one as a central focus will help you get started. Look into your past for formative experiences. Is there something that happened that changed your life? That shaped your values? A memorable adventure? Is there a person who deeply affected you?

As mentioned earlier, this could be an unhappy experience. Writing about it might be uncomfortable at first, but you'll probably find that the essay will help you come to terms with it. In fact, many authors say they need to write in order to make sense of the world.

Here is a brief list of topics appropriate for a personal essay. Notice how they all fall into the category of a person (animals, too!), place or event:

- a pet dog or cat
- a favorite teacher
- a treehouse
- a swingset
- an adventure
- a hike or boating trip
- memories of a relative
- learning to play an instrument
- moving into a new house
- fishing for the first time
- first day at school
- getting stitches

Now, when it comes to topics, keep a few warnings in mind. Like all essays, you want a narrow and appropriate topic. Don't write about all six members of your family, or every experience you've ever had at summer camp since your were five! You also want an experience that is accessible. If it's too subjective, esoteric, or revelatory, you run the risk of losing the reader either by distancing or offending him. Ultimately, of course, it's a matter of how well your experience is communicated.

Also note that your topic, while succinct, does not have to be limited by time or place. In fact, some of the richest subjects are attended to as they evolve in time. Perhaps there was a beautiful pine tree in your neighborhood park. When you were a little kid you climbed it, played games on it; when you were a little older, you would read under its shade. As you grew older, you forgot about the tree, only to find out that it's been cut down. How are you going to recapture the richness of that tree? Is it a metaphor for your own growth? Is its disappearance symbolic of your vanished childhood? In order to communicate this, you would highlight the passages of life, centering on the tree throughout.

Developing your topic

Brainstorming for the details of a personal essay is a very rich experience. Once you tap the fertile ground of your memories, you can open up old diaries, call up relatives and friends, look through photo albums, watch family videos, and so forth. You just might start remembering happenings you hadn't recalled in years.

Suppose you're going to write about your favorite uncle, John. He lives in Oregon, where you have visited him every summer since you were a child. Your memories of these visits are very rich. Why not have a cup of tea with some family members and share memories of Uncle John? The hope here (in addition to having fun) is to unearth some colorful material, to find connections and themes.

What if Uncle John had a habit of leaving his glasses on his dinner plate, and they always ended up in the kitchen sink? And yet when it came to organization and tidiness, he was the most meticulous man you ever met! You thought you were the only one who noticed this! Now that you think of it, could he have been doing this on purpose? Given his quirkiness, it certainly wouldn't be beyond him.

Now that you've assembled your details, they should start to take shape, to move towards the central focus of your essay. Remember, you're not simply writing down memories. As you continue to collect details, consider what the driving point of your essay will be. Maybe you never realized that what you treasure about Uncle John is his combination of mischievousness and tenderness.

In addition to details, you should be brainstorming the variety of feelings you have towards the subject. Is there a bittersweet nostalgia? Resentment? Gratitude? Sadness? Joy? A mixture of feelings? The overriding feeling will play into your choice of tone and style. However, it's likely you won't know exactly how you feel until you write the essay. It bears repeating: *What you already know about your topic is the starting point of your personal essay. By writing about it you will be making discoveries.* When we say 'discoveries', we don't necessarily mean something dramatic. Your discovery might simply be a new way to look at something, or the ability to articulate it: It's Uncle John's *tender mischievousness* that you want to write about.

Structuring your essay

While the personal essay involves narrative writing (or storytelling), it's important to remember that it has the same—or even more challenging—structural demands as any other essay. Remember, a personal essay is not a diary entry. Rather, there is a central meaning, something the paper is aiming towards. To call it a thesis might be helpful, but 'thesis' implies the need to argue or prove a point. Here we're dealing more with a clear focus, a discovery. Therefore, it's important that every memory you highlight relates to that central focus. The choices you make in your outline, therefore, are very important. They will ensure that you don't digress.

The structure is, however, more flexible than most essays. In fact, you can be as creative with structure as you want, as long as it works! How to tell? That's a writer's choice—you'll know. Is it balanced? Does it come together intelligibly? Staying with Uncle John, you'll probably want to begin by writing a standard outline. Let's say you choose three memorable events about Uncle John, events that illustrate his personality. Now you can experiment with how best to order these memories.

For example, why not begin by writing about the last time you saw him?

> He sits quietly reading, his legs crossed, his face hidden behind the newspaper as he rocks gently on the porch swing. I throw a few more suitcases into the car, then turn around and walk back to the house. As I near the door, Uncle John slowly lowers the paper until his eyes peer out just for a moment—enough for that mischievous look, and then he hides behind the newspaper again.

Using this as an introduction, you can now move back to childhood and recreate an important event that highlights John's personality. You'll be able to guide the reader along with transitions:

> The first time I was introduced to the squinty, smiling grey eyes was in the summer of 1989, when we drove 15 hours to Uncle John and Aunt Claire's house. We pulled up and there he was, in full fishing regalia, rods in hand, ready for adventure. The only trouble was, I hated fishing.

Notice how the theme is picked up on and the next account begins naturally. It's like moving from topic to topic in any other essay. Also, notice how we started in the present and moved to the past. There are many variations of this. As long as you don't confuse the reader, as long as the paper establishes some kind of *internal logic*, you're free to experiment.

After two more episodes, for example, we might return to the image of Uncle John on the porch swing, and you're about to return home. Instead of a mischievous look in his eye, you notice tears of sadness—his tender nature.

In our case, describing three Uncle John episodes will be enough. You don't want to fill the essay with too many experiences. Be careful not to overload the reader.

As you can tell, an outline comes in handy. While it might be a bit looser than a formal outline, it should provide the spine for your paper so that your paper is balanced and not rambling.

WRITING YOUR PAPER

Now that you've got a sound structure and wonderful details, how are you going to translate your personal feelings? This is a difficult question to answer because there is no one right way. Finding a voice for a personal narrative is a challenge because you want to remain intimate yet accessible. *You might have to start writing in order to discover how you want to write about your topic.* One helpful exercise is to write the opening paragraph in a number of different styles. This will give you choices—you'll know which one is right for you. Still, there are some demands particular to the personal essay, along with some pitfalls to avoid. Here are some tips that will help guide you in the right direction.

(1) **Show, don't tell**. This one sounds familiar, doesn't it? We revisit the golden rule of writing here because a personal essay, perhaps more than any other essay, relies on being illustrative and avoiding generalities. "Gosh, Uncle John was such a nice guy. He was really mischievous but he loved us a lot," won't do. Haven't we all had the experience of driving through a friend's home town, hearing about the significance of every doughnut shop? Boring, isn't it? Why? Because you can't relate to their experience, because there's no immediacy to it, nothing to draw you in. They're telling you *about* their trip rather than bringing you with them.

Remember, then, not to let your essay become a slide show. You want to use vivid details, to create specific scenes. When writing about a **place**, bring it to life through descriptions of its setting. When describing an **event**, present it fully, allowing the action to propel the event forward. Use dialogue sparingly, only when it's purposeful. When describing a **person**, let the reader see her face, the tone of her voice, the way she walks. In all cases, you have the freedom to be subjective, to use imaginative language. Here's our favorite uncle again:

> When he fishes he resembles a statue, though a closer look shows that he's relaxed. His face is calm, his tanned and wrinkled summer cheeks drooping a little as his grey eyes meditate on the water. When he's like this there's an unspoken code: It's time for fishing and quiet. Until he gets a bite, Uncle John has disappeared.

(2) **Let the discovery unfold**. When someone tells you the end of a movie, it's spoiled, isn't it? The screenplay is written and the movie directed so that the scenes will unfold and the audience will feel the power of the ending. The same is true with your writing. The reader must be involved with the spirit and movement of the piece throughout the entire paper. This is why it's so important not to tell the reader what you're feeling, but to have him experience it with you.

Which of these paragraphs does a better job of allowing you into the moment? Which one is more like a drive through a friend's hometown?

> When I opened my presents I bit my lip and tried to hide my disappointment: Uncle John gave me a keychain for my ninth birthday! Fifteen minutes later, he got into his old blue Chevy and started the engine. Was something wrong? Did I make him mad? Suddenly, he honked and I saw that gleam in his eye. He pointed to a bulky object covered by a blue sheet on the side of the front porch. I walked over and slid the sheet off. There it was, a beautiful two-story, handmade doll house!

> I remember when Uncle John gave me a keychain for my ninth birthday, only to surprise me fifteen minutes later with a beautiful two story, hand-made doll house. Earlier, when presents were opened, he had given me the keychain in order to trick me. I bit my lip and tried to hide my disappointment. But when he got into his old blue Chevy, he honked and I saw that gleam in his eye. He pointed to a bulky object covered by a blue sheet on the side of the front porch. I walked over and slid the sheet off. There it was, a beautiful two-story, handmade doll house!

The second paragraph gives away the surprise, and the details lose their impact. The reader is not included in the suspense. In the first example, there's tension; we are as surprised as the girl in the story. It's good writing.

(3) **Keep the writing immediate**. Again, we have a common rule of writing that takes on special importance with the personal essay. Because you're writing from memory, retelling an account, it's easy to slip into the habit of using words and phrases like "I remember," "once," "when we used to," and so forth. These phrases are sometimes necessary, but if they are overused they distance the reader from the essay. In this paragraph, notice how these "recollection" phrases fill the sentences with fluff:

> We used to go miniature golfing a lot. I remember one time when Uncle John came along with us, and how he golfed so many funny ways. Once, he used the back of the club. Another time he used his club like it was a pool stick. I remember thinking this was pretty funny.

Not only are we being told Uncle John's antics are funny, but the writing is labored with remembering.

(4) **Always remember you're writing for an audience**. Because this is so important, it bears repeating. If your content or writing style is intimate and deeply subjective, then it's your duty to keep it accessible. You must be able to reach an attentive reader. Once you're done with your first draft, try to become objective about your essay—read it with new eyes. Does it assume too much on the reader's part? Are there inside jokes? Have you helped the reader care about your subject?

READING WARM-UP

(A) Study the student essay on page 85, "Learning to Bow," by Nao Braverman. Share your impressions with classmates. How does Nao reach the reader? What kinds of images and episodes are highlighted? What discovery surfaces in the essay? Is the writing clear? Enter your impressions in your reading journal.

(B) Read several personal essays or passages from autobiographies. Go through the features of writing, looking attentively for the strategies we covered. Enter your responses in your journal.

WRITING WARM-UP

Write one page describing a vivid childhood scene in as much detail as possible.

GROUP LEARNING

Read your one page childhood scene out loud to a group. See whether they have questions about the experience. Do these questions point to some details you should have provided? Are they moved by the power of your writing? Are they touched by the experience itself?

Learning to Bow
by Nao Braverman

As I sat quietly on the tatami floor, my parents closed the door behind them, leaving me in an unfamiliar room with a family whose lifestyle and customs I had yet to learn. The summer before my first year in high school, I decided to experience a part of the Japanese culture outside of the small temple village where my grandparents lived. So instead of paying the regular visit to relatives in Sakai, my mother's home town, for two weeks I stayed with a friend in Tokyo and attended high school classes with her. As I sat at the dinner table on the night of my arrival, I felt a mixture of excitement and unease.

The next morning, I awoke energetic, ready to begin my first day at school. With extreme precision, my friend Megumi helped me into a sailor's style blouse, stiff pleated skirt, and penny loafers. The royal blue scarf had to be tied right side over left around my neck; the skirt had to be knee length—not higher, not lower. Everything had to be exactly coordinated, right down to the color of my undershirt. Absolutely no accessories, no makeup. At first I thought I was attending a strict private school, but later I learned that these restrictions applied to almost all Japanese schools. We ate a quick breakfast of rice and miso soup and hurried out the door. It was then that I first encountered rush hour in Japan.

When we say "rush hour" here in California, we mean that exasperating experience of trying to drive to work at the same time as thousands of others. Here, too many cars try to get on the same road. In Japan, too many people try to get on the same train. As soon as I purchased my ticket, I felt myself being swept forward by an incredible mass of humanity. I had never seen so many people clustered together in such a small space! As the blur of suits, briefcases, and school uniforms filled my vision, I nervously scanned the array of bobbing heads for my friend's black pony tail, but there were too many like it. Just as I was beginning to panic, I felt someone gently push me in the direction of a train that had just arrived. As soon as the sliding doors of the empty train had barely parted, people were pouring in. In a matter of seconds the cars were so full that the people on the sides were pushed up against the walls, and yet many more were still boarding. I was shocked when Megumi directed me to this train, which already looked like it was about to collapse. She taught me how to step on backwards so that I could squeeze myself in. Finally, the door slid closed and my shoulder was pressed against the windowpane. I could feel an elbow sticking into my lower back, and the little air there was smelled like a mixture of the dry cleaners and cigarette smoke.

Later, I found myself in a crowded classroom filled with the clicking of penny loafers against a shiny linoleum floor and the noisy chatter of teenagers. But as soon as the teacher entered the room, the students fell silent and moved quietly to the seats. I pulled out my chair to sit down when I noticed that the students were standing quietly behind their desks. Megumi gestured for me to remain standing. A student in the first row shouted, "Stand up straight!" and then "Bow!" Then students bowed in unison and I followed their motions. The teacher in front bowed to us in return. "Sit down!" yelled the student, and we sat. This ritual felt awkward at first, but I soon became accustomed to it.

There were many rules and customs for me to learn, but the ones most difficult to retain were those involving behavior and etiquette. No one would tell me outright whether my manners were poor, so I was forced to rely on my own judgment. Fortunately, it was in my nature to observe those around me and adapt to their behavior, but I still missed some important rules. I learned that "maybe" meant "yes" sometimes and "no" at other times, and that it was rude to express selfish desires. I learned to bow several times and say, "I am intruding" when I entered another's house. I learned to deny compliments and to put myself down constantly. I learned to always bring people gifts, and to refuse gifts presented to me. I learned to smile and sit quietly and smile and sit quietly.

Parting with Megumi in Tokyo was sad and lonely. But as soon as I walked out the door after thanking, bowing, and apologizing several times, I caught myself breathing a sigh of relief. Although I had thoroughly enjoyed the experience, at that moment I felt as though I had been holding my breath and clenching my teeth for the past two weeks. I realized how stressful it had been trying to adapt so quickly to a different culture.

I was exhausted, yet I felt enriched. I had learned more about my mother's culture and about myself. I could picture my mother in a stiff uniform and penny loafers, rushing to catch the early train. I connected many of my character traits to my mother's traditional upbringing. I had always had difficulty expressing desire, and I always apologized a little too much. These habits I now recognized as proper manners in the Japanese culture.

The Mock Essay:
Learning through Imitation

After reading one of your favorite writers, have you ever found yourself imitating his style? Suddenly your sentences are longer, your paragraphs more varied, your tone a bit unfamiliar? This is natural. In fact, most writers will tell you that part of developing their own styles involved (consciously or not) imitation. Others develop their own niche *by purposely* imitating writing styles.

Writing a mock essay can mean one of two things. First, you can simply imitate an essayist. All writers have habits and qualities. To imitate a writer well you have to study her style, and that's always beneficial. We will cover this in depth below.

The second approach is to write a "pretend" essay. Your job here is to make up an essay by assuming authority on a subject (whether you have it or not!) along with a false persona, or a voice other than your own. To put it simply, you are pretending to be someone else! For example, you might be a Civil War nurse writing about her experiences in a hospital. You could also be a historian comparing and contrasting two wars that never occurred. The possibilities are limitless. Here you have more license to create than in an imitation essay.

This is a challenging assignment. If attended to wholeheartedly, it offers a lot of rewards, including a great deal of enjoyment. Because you won't be using your own voice or writing style, *you'll be forced to stretch yourself, to see new possibilities*. We can all use this, as it's very easy to get bogged down and habituated.

ASSIGNMENT

Write a three-to-five-page double-spaced mock essay.

By either imitating an established writer or making up an essay, your goal is to compose a piece that reads like a formal essay.

FINDING A TOPIC AND AN APPROACH

For the imitation essay, begin by choosing a writer. We're limiting ourselves to writers of nonfiction. Most students like to mimic a writer whose style they find overboard, someone they can have fun with. Of course, you might not want your imitation to be mimicry, but a straightforward attempt at capturing the writer's style.

The other approach, the "pretend" essay, has numerous faces. First of all, decide on the nature of the piece you're writing. Will it be an editorial? A historical essay? Don't limit yourself to the kinds of essays covered in this book. What about an interpretive piece on *Pride and Prejudice?* As long as it's an essay, anything is fair game. Here are just a few possibilities:

- an academic presentation on the connection between biodiversity and trading cards
- an editorial in favor of paying collegiate student athletes
- an acceptance speech for a glamorous award
- an inaugural speech
- a mock historical document
- an interpretive paper on the importance of Snoopy in American culture
- a research paper on the history of the roller coaster
- an introduction to the collected works of a fictitious writer

As you can see, there is a lot of territory here, and lots more available. However, along with that freedom are the choices and the limitations that follow. Take the question of audience, for example. If you're writing a mock high school graduation keynote address pretending to be a famous alum, your audience consists of the school staff, the graduates, and their family members. You would write with the intention of reaching them. Or let's suppose you're pretending to be an astronomer who just discovered a new planet in the constellation Cassiopeia. Where are you going to submit this essay? Probably to a scientific journal, right? Your immediate audience will consist of like-minded astronomers who will need convincing.

Once you've settled on subject matter and an audience, the question of *voice* and *persona* surfaces. While you're free to make up facts and direct quotes, your voice needs to be specific and consistent. Who are you? Well, that's where the fun comes in. In our case, one would assume the keynote speaker is someone of social stature, a senator perhaps. Given the parameters and themes of such speeches, this senator is likely to fill his speech with platitudes about making a difference in the world, quotes from Abraham Lincoln, and so on. Most likely, there will be a formal, lofty tone:

> Graduates of the class of 1999, esteemed staff and parents, I am most honored and humbled to address you on this momentous occasion, this rite of passage into adulthood. You young people sitting before me represent the future of this great nation. I would like to take a moment to explore what it means to be a citizen, to think about your great duties as you enter the frontier of college and beyond.

Sound familiar? The passage grabs the general spirit of many commencement addresses: the emphasis on responsibility, the future, and so forth. This is not a mocking passage, but these sentiments can easily be exaggerated if that's to your liking. Another option is to contrast the flavor of the piece against what's expected. What if the commencement speaker surprised everyone?

> Dear graduates, esteemed staff members, and family, I am honored to be here speaking with you. However, I must admit I have nothing profound to say, no advice I can give that will be helpful, no great wisdom to pass on, nobody to quote for inspiration. You kids sitting there with those caps and gowns, you'll take your beatings in life, but everyone does, so just keep pushing through. Be kind to people. Besides that, enjoy life.

Pretty different, eh? The passage has a touch of personality and humor. Again, though, it should be emphasized that your essay doesn't have to be humorous, or mocking in its spirit. It can be an attempt to imitate a lofty commencement speech. As long as you maintain a consistent voice and persona, pick whichever style works for you.

If you're writing an imitation piece, an amusing variation is to have a famous writer adopt unfamiliar territory. Again, it's a play on contrasts. For example, could you imagine Ralph Waldo Emerson, a great essayist known for his lofty and abstract meditations on life, writing about the art of vacuuming? Here are a few lines of the real Emerson:

> Nature is made to conspire with spirit to emancipate us. Certain mechanical changes, a small alteration in our local position, apprizes us of a dualism. We are strangely affected by seeing the shore from a moving ship, from a balloon, or through the tints of an unusual sky. The least change in our point of view gives the whole world a pictorial air.
>
> —From "Nature," by Ralph Waldo Emerson

This gives you a taste of Emerson's style. Notice the elevated, poetic language, the abstractions, and the authority. Now let's play with the subject matter:

> When one endeavors to vacuum, be it a bedroom, hallway, or living room, one's spirit should be localized on the carpet, on the shifting landscapes within its realm. The parallel movements should be of primary importance for a sense of natural order to occur, like the waves of the sea lapping the shore or the melting snow of a distant precipice.

Notice how strange the Emersonian style sounds when writing about something as mundane as vacuuming. Still, his voice is captured. A few words and phrases are borrowed, images are created, rhythms are copied. And interestingly enough, imitating his style gives a whole different flavor to the "art" of vacuuming, doesn't it? This teaches us a great lesson about writing: It's not so much what you write, but *how* you write that counts.

Developing your paper

By now, the variety of approaches to the mock essay should be clear. You should also have an idea of the writing choices you have to make. If you're imitating a writer, take the following steps *before* you begin writing. They will let you tune in to the writer's voice and style. **Note**: Pick one essay as a model for these exercises. This will help maintain consistency.

(1) **Copy a page of the essay by hand**. This will help you directly experience the writer's style: sentence variety, word choice, and so forth. Stay focused while you do this exercise. It pays off!

(2) **Study the writing tendencies, including word choice , punctuation, grammar, etc.** All writer's have tendencies, and it's these you'll want to feature in the imitation piece. Can you uncover some of the writer's favorite words or unusual phrases? Does she use the word *infallible* too often? Is his vernacular loaded with polysyllabic words? Does she use parentheses often? Too many rhetorical questions? Does he move from concrete detail to metaphor in one sentence? As you can see, there's a wonderful opportunity to look at the complexity of writing choices that we studied in the first part of this book. It's also a great way to extend your vocabulary.

(3) **Practice imitating the writer's voice**. This is the most challenging part of the imitation. Even though you have the language and writing style down, there's something illusive about a genuine voice, something that perhaps cannot ever truly be imitated. As an experiment, write a few imitation paragraphs on subjects that your writer would adopt. Hand them, along with some of the writer's real work, to a classmate. See whether your classmate can tell the difference.

When it comes to "inventing" an essay, you need to follow the same steps as you would in any other essay: brainstorm details, prepare an outline, watch for digression, remain focused, and so on. As mentioned earlier, you're free to make up your own facts, statistics, and direct quotes—just be sure that they maintain internal consistency. If you're going for informality throughout, then keep it up. Here's the closing of our second commencement speech:

Let me say I'm sorry I didn't have any fortune cookies to hand out or crystal balls to see through. I've always found that you have gotta live things through yourself. I always wanted to drive an ice cream truck—you know, the ones that jingle around neighborhoods. It would be so nice to see the kids running with happy looks on their faces. I never did it because I wanted to "be somebody." I think I'll go buy that truck now. Thanks for listening.

Structuring your essay

Now that you've nailed down your approach and are comfortable with your persona and voice, it's time to structure your paper. The imitation essay can be structured by simply imitating the model essay you're using. Sticking with Emerson's "Nature," you would uncover the structure of his essay and follow it in yours. If it helps, write a formal outline for his essay. (You'll have to trim down the volume, as his work is quite long.) The other option is to write an outline as you would for any other paper—as long as it remains similar to the writer's approach. Emerson, for instance, often used subheadings to develop his points. You would want to imitate this.

The structural demands of a "pretend" essay vary, depending on the type of essay you're writing. An introduction to a book will be different than an editorial in a small town newspaper, right? Do all scholarly essays have footnotes? Returning to our example, find several commencement speeches. How many of them open with some kind of anecdote? How long are they? Be sure to do your homework. This will ensure the believability you're looking for.

WRITING YOUR PAPER

Whether you're writing an imitation piece or a "pretend" essay, your particular challenge here is to capture a persona and a style that *remains consistent.* Watch carefully for your own speaking and writing tendencies creeping into the prose. Here's our formal commencement speaker again, wrapping up his address:

And thus our citizenry is modeled after our forefathers' vision of a country of self-sufficient, self-ruling individuals who strive for independence while remaining responsible for the whole. You students of Smith High are those citizens, and don't you know it! So when you move on to college or a job, remember that it's really your duty to restore the ideals of this nation. Thank you.

"And don't you know it" doesn't fit here; it's a slang phrase that the formal speaker wouldn't use. Also, consider the use of the intensifier *really*. Does that seem natural?

As long as you establish consistency, you're all set. Employ everything you know about the writing process and have fun!

READING WARM-UP

(A) Study the student essay on page 94, *"The Best of the Shaggy Floater Group* Album Liner Notes," by Dan Helfman. Share your impressions with classmates. What is the spirit of the paper? Is it believable? Are there particularly humorous passages? What's the tone of the piece? Is the writing good? Enter your impressions in your reading journal.

(B) Review some of the the essays you've read so far—those you have liked and those you didn't like. One of these might provide the model for your essay.

(C) Read a few published mock essays. Ask a librarian or teacher for help in finding them.

WRITING WARM-UP

(A) Before writing your essay, practice imitating the styles of several writers. If you have been reading essays together with a group, read your imitation aloud. Can people identify the writer?

(B) Imitate **your own** writing style! Can you see your own tendencies? Take them and exaggerate them.

GROUP LEARNING

Perhaps you've become familiar with some of your classmates' writing styles. Have someone shuffle a group of essays together and hand them out randomly. Each person takes an essay and rewrites a few passages, exaggerating the writer's style.

The Best of the Shaggy Floater Group Album Liner Notes
by Dan Helfman

When producer Abdul Jamal Goldberg reluctantly signed a most peculiar little blues guitarist named Shaggy Floater for a recording contract with Los Angeles-based Cool Cat Records, he didn't have any idea he was launching the career of a monumental figure in jazz history during the latter half of the twentieth century, a figure to stand with the likes of Satchmo, Duke, Dizzy, Bird, Miles, and Trane. Through his unsurpassed guitar work and unforgettable vocals, Shaggy continued the best traditions of those innovators and created many of his own in the process. Every member of the Shaggy Floater Group had a similar effect upon the genre. Portly Chessman, Luther Lamont Jefferson, Cherry Morello, and Shaggy's numerous other collaborators created a new image of jazz, a new way of looking at this marvelous form of music. With their delightfully zany compositions and innovations, they revealed the grandly understated artistry of jazz to the unsuspecting public. "I didn't know what hit me," said the noted sousaphone player Bubba Mac when he first heard the group perform. That was basically the response of the entire world. True, the band had its roots deeply planted in classic jazz traditions, but it was also very different.

Born to a preacher father and schoolteacher mother, Shaggy spent most of his youth in Chicago. Perhaps it was listening to his father's vast collection of blues records that encouraged Shaggy to acquire a taste for the blues at an early age. By the time he was five he had already taken up guitar as more than a pastime. "Just always had a knack for it. My thing from the beginning," he says in retrospect. Noticed by some talent scouts at his elementary school, by the age of ten Shaggy was jamming in Windy City nightclubs and bars with such notables as Slippery Rivers and His Band. In high school, Shaggy started his own blues group, Shaggy F. and the Mothers, named for the fact that he was the sole young man in the band—the rest were older women. They were popular for quite a while, once even touring the nation. It was at this time that Shaggy first cultivated his trademark outlandish music and dress style. The Mothers lasted through Shaggy's college days until it disbanded after tensions amongst the members became unbearable. Angered by his band's demise, he began to miss recording sessions and failed to appear at certain performance venues. For several months, he even refused to touch his beloved guitar, Rochelle.

During this period, Shaggy impulsively wandered across the country, often taking bus trips to New York and back. These long, grim excursions left a deep impression on him, and served as inspiration to write "Dat's Da Bus Station Blues," which would become one of his group's signature themes, as you'll hear on this compilation. Shaggy finally settled in New York. He quit playing night gigs, but gave occasional day performances in Manhattan coffee houses, a job which he despised. These annoying concerts proved fruitful, however, because at one of them he met the renowned jazz vocalist Chili Blackbean. She became enthralled by his playing and immediately took him under her wing. Introducing him to more elegant forms of jazz, Chili brought him to the West Coast and introduced him to Goldberg, who was put off by this strange man, but later changed his mind when he heard Shaggy play. He immediately gave him a contract with Cool Cat.

In the early years of his career with Cool Cat, Shaggy mainly recorded with Chili and the Evan Dill Orchestra. They produced several popular albums, including the chart-topping *Meet Mister Handsome Devil*. Written and sung by Chili, the title tune featured a long solo by Shaggy that solidified his reputation. His blues guitar and mumbled singing were interesting counterparts to Chili's relaxed vocals and the Orchestra's swinging sounds. After Shaggy's success with the the song, "The Girl From Tijuana," on *Sketches of Baja*, composer-band leader Evan Dill said Shaggy should start his own group. With that advice, Shaggy set about the task of beginning the Shaggy Floater Group. He recruited other Cool Cat personalities as well as veteran players from the Orchestra. There were several incarnations of the band before the classic group was formed with Portly Chessman on piano, Luther Lamont Jefferson on bass, and Cherry Morello on drums. The world of jazz would never be the same.

Indeed, the classic Shaggy Floater Group has a unique lineup. Portly, a classically trained pianist from Ghana, emulates the gentle styles of Bill Evans and Oscar Peterson. A man of great elegance and culture known for his frequent patronage of the arts, Portly has striven over the years not to be lured into the world of drugs as his friends and colleagues had. Bass player Luther Lamont hails from the Hell's Kitchen area in New York. Early in his long career, he adapted the fiery-toned solos of black East Coast jazzmen. Tired of the city, Luther Lamont headed to the West Coast and cultivated an interesting hybrid personality: the dress style and laid-back quality of the 1950's cool players with a 1960's hard bop bass sound. Cherry, a fantastic drummer from Kansas, has unreasonably been the victim of scandalous tabloid headlines with regard to her "questionable" herbal teas. The senior member of the group should not be underestimated in any way; she tosses off complicated polyrhythmic lines that would be difficult for someone thirty years her junior. Cherry has most definitely carved a niche for herself in jazz history. Together, this gifted group has created a landmark association.

In its first years, the Shaggy Floater Group recorded with many collaborators, varying the personnel with every performance. Chili introduced Shaggy to Cool Cat veterans such as tenor saxophonist Pharaoh Ra, famous for his exceedingly difficult composition, "Vast Strides," which became another of the group's signature themes heard here; trumpeter Cheeks Mitchell, a longtime member of the Evan Dill Orchestra; and vibraphone virtuoso Jade, an ex-folk musician whose accompaniment gave the band a decidedly whimsical quality. Their first well-known album was *Old Chestnuts and Young Whippersnappers*, a collection of standard pieces. It was very successful, and with it began the group's tradition of having at least one standard on each recording. Their next album, *Shaggy Floats*, introduced some of their famous tunes to the world, including Shaggy's funky "You Got That Right," "Dat's Da Bus Station Blues," and Cherry's "Rayon Negligee." *Wagon Train* featured the catchy title cut inspired by American frontier ballads, Luther Lamont's mostly solo "Touching Bass," and Mitchell's popular "Cheeks and Balances." With three albums under their belts, the group began a tour of the globe. They produced a few live concert recordings with Chili that reprised "Meet Mister Handsome Devil" and "The Girl From Tijuana." Meanwhile, Portly composed and recorded the score for the espionage thriller, *Downtown Express Operative*. As successful as they had been, however, their most influential period was yet to come.

When the group returned from its tour, it took an extended hiatus. Over the course of that year, Portly and Jade collaborated to write several tunes, particularly the folk-jazz piece "Calypso Facto," later to become a group standard. It is clear that the two of them worked together very well, because shortly thereafter they were married, and have remained so since. Shaggy and Portly also got together that summer to write "Mojo Fo' Me, If You Please," and the classic, gospel-inspired "Says Right Here." Gathering a year's worth of tunes, Shaggy asked the group to meet again for a new album, *Shades of Blue*. The group members came completely unrehearsed to the Cool Cat recording studio and were met by Shaggy, who had drawn a series of skeleton charts left wide open for improvisation. Within a week they had successfully recorded all of the pieces. Most of the final cuts were first takes. Everything about the album fit neatly into place. It represented a "personal best" for the group, and the album went on to go platinum. The celebrated tunes on this legendary album are now standards in every modern jazz musician's repertoire.

Shaggy used some of the proceeds from *Shades of Blue* to open the Shaggy Floater Institute, an academy designed to encourage aspiring young musicians to reach their potential in the world of jazz. A multitude of talented young people have already graduated from the Institute, and countless more will benefit from its influence. Members of the Shaggy Floater Group teach there on a regular basis so as to "pass the baton." This compilation represents the very best of the group's playing. Even now, the group continues to play and innovate jazz, and will hopefully do so for many more years to come.

—Leo Boa, March, 1998

Answer Key

REWRITING AWKWARD SENTENCES, page 25 (Answers may vary)

(A)

1. A lunar eclipse occurs when the earth moves in front of the sun, casting a shadow on the moon.
2. It took a long time to rebuild our home after it was damaged by the earthquake.
3. In my town, Spanish style houses blend into the landscape more than others.
4. As she jumped rope with great style and speed, the crowd cheered her on.
5. In his attempt to cook the lasagna, he caused it to burn to a charcoal.
6. I know so many people whose friends double as their worst enemies.
7. The happiest times of life are made possible by good friendships.
8. Despite their attempts to get the crowd at the football game to recycle cans and bottles, the students had to dig them out of the trash can anyway.
9. A utopia is a perfect civilization.
10. In one powerful leap, the graceful mountain goat caused the avalanche.

(B)

1. He told me that his relationship to his coach was a struggle.
2. For his children's sake, he decided not to sell his home.
3. When I started high school, I thought I should start considering my profession.
4. We were discussing which is better: being rich or poor.
5. The Middle East peace process is another major issue in the news.
6. In volleyball, a spike occurs when a player leaps and slams the ball over the net.
7. She tells him he should pray—especially when he's uncertain about his decision.
8. Take care of yourself before you get sick, instead of waiting until you're sick and then taking medicine.
9. He thinks there is nothing that he can't do.
10. The airplane ran out of gas and the pilot looked for a place to land.

(C)

1. In the most surprising and honest ways, he tries to solve the callers' problems.
2. Like so many deer hunters, my weapon of choice is the rifle.
3. Traveling, especially to big cities, is definitely not on his list of fun.
4. The note says to call 911.
5. My interest in skateboarding helped determine the type of friends I had.
6. Butterflies in the stomach and a dry throat are common for most people in these situations.
7. The explosions were bigger and more life-like, and the new scenes were blended into the movie magnificently.
8. One man said that the low wages they earn as day laborers are more than they would make in Mexico.
9. Looking at the photos, I see that they truly reflect the panic I was feeling.
10. I attended private school from first through fourth grade.

Answer Key (cont.)

(D)

1. The reason his coarse brown hair stays in perfect form is clear: He applies handfuls of gel every morning.
2. Ernie attempts to imitate his dog's well-known curled lip by contorting his upper lip slightly while his lower lip slides to the left.
3. Using his hand as his microphone, and screaming at the top of his lungs, he sings every word slightly off-key.
4. But wait! I can't stop now; after all, I've come so far.
5. Weathering the extreme desert heat, I became moody.
6. A pulsing sensation like an electric shock ran through her body when she felt the pull of the fishing pole.
7. The night grows late, and the morning grows early, bringing with it the chirping of birds and the crowing of roosters.
8. Each flake, so intricate and unique, whirled as it fell and then settled into deep powdery drifts.
9. He's a bit skinny. Well, more than a bit—he's a bean pole.
10. The lady possesses high self-esteem and strong motivation.

QUOTE INCORPORATION, page 34 (Answers may vary)

1. When Willa Cather opens *O Pioneers!*, she says, "One January day...the little town of Hanover, anchored on a windy Nebraska tableland, was trying not to be blown away."
2. Willa Cather's *O Pioneers!* opens with an appropriate description of landscape: "One January day...."
3. "One January day, thirty years ago," writes Willa Cather in the opening of *O Pioneers!*, "the little town of Hanover...was trying not to be blown away."
4. "One January day, thirty years ago, the little town of Hanover...was trying not to be blown away," writes Willa Cather in *O Pioneers!*
5. In *O Pioneers!*, Willa Cather writes about the hardships that take place in "the little town of Hanover, anchored on a windy Nebraska tableland."

SENTENCE COMBINING, page 38 (Answers may vary)

(A)

1-2. The pizza is on the living room table.

3-4. India is an ancient country where many dialects are spoken.

5-7. The thirsty ants are coming single file into our kitchen.

8-10. Computers are very useful because you can keep records on them and use the Internet, too.

Answer Key (cont.)

(B)

1-2. Jerusalem is a sacred city in Israel.

3-5. There are Jewish, Christian, and Muslim holy places.

6-8. Many religious seekers travel from all over the world to Jerusalem's synagogues, churches and mosques.

9-10. Many civilizations have occupied Jerusalem, including Babylonian, Roman, and Ottoman.

11-13. The most sacred Jewish site is the Western Wall, a piece of King Solomon's Temple, which was destroyed by the Romans in A.D. 70.

14-16. There are many Christian sites in and around Jerusalem, including The Way of Sorrows, which is believed to be the route Jesus walked before the Crucifixion.

17-19. The central Muslim site is the Dome of the Rock, a beautiful, colorful mosque that is believed to stand on the spot where Mohammed made his mystical flight to heaven.

RELATIVE CLAUSES, page 41 (Answers may vary)

(A)

1-2. I might fill in for Mark, <u>who is going on a trip to Europe</u>.

3-4. The pillow, <u>which is very soft and comfortable</u>, is the largest in our house.

5-7. Queen Elizabeth of England, <u>whose history is chronicled in many books</u>, signed the death warrant of Mary Queen of Scots and saw the defeat of the Spanish Armada.

8-9. Herman Melville, <u>who is known for his stories of adventure on the seas</u>, wrote *Moby Dick* in 1851.

10-12. Isaac's lollipop, <u>which was missing</u>, was found sticking to a cushion in the sofa.

(B)

1-4. The tourists, <u>who came from all over the nation</u>, gathered at the shore to watch the slim and sleek speed boats.

5-7. The boats, <u>which raced in twos</u>, made a full circle around some buoys <u>that were more than a mile apart</u>.

8-9. My dad, <u>whose favorite boat was called *Jackknife*</u>, cheered like a madman.

10-12. *Jackknife*, <u>which was leading the race</u>, failed when its engine caught fire and the driver jumped overboard.

(C)

1-2. We took a train trip across the United States <u>that was about 3,000 miles long</u>.

3-6. My friends, <u>who were tired</u>, slept through the first part of the trip through the California desert, <u>which I found beautiful</u>.

7-8. When we passed through the Great Plains, <u>which I found boring</u>, we played cards.

Answer Key (cont.)

9-10. Sheila, whose backpack was missing, was very unhappy by the time we reached the East Coast.

11-14. "I must have left it at the crowded depot in St. Louis, which is the last place I remember seeing it," she said.

PARTICIPIAL PHRASES, page 44

A)

1. Walking down the street, she noticed the overcast sky.
2. Blushing, the bride walked down the aisle.
3. Mandated by the government, we bought a pass to go into the wilderness.
4. Whispering a political speech, the five-year-old amazed the onlookers.
5. Mr. Pilwinker, attempting to inspire the students, gave an impassioned speech.
6. I ran around to the back of the house when the lightning, striking with increased frequency, nearly hit me.
7. The flag, torn by the wind, was hanging like a rag.
8. The zebras walked out of the zoo unnoticed by the trainers.
9. Thrashing across the Atlantic, the hurricane hit North Carolina with ferocity.
10. The coffee, scalding my fingers, is too hot to drink.

(B) (Answers may vary)

1-2. The team, excited about the bowling match, had been practicing all month.

3-5. The orange balloon, floating away, was followed by a curious sea gull.

6-7. Riding in the car, the baby fell asleep.

8-9. Bored, I went star gazing this evening and I saw Jupiter!

10-12. The customer, insisting that she exchange 10,000 pennies for one hundred dollars, demanded to see the bank manager.

(C) (Answers may vary)

1-3. Excited, Paula brought the brand new computer home.

4-5. Plugging in the computer, Paula realized that she didn't know how to turn it on.

6-7. Disappointed, she read the instruction manual.

8-9. Thumbing through the pages, she discovered that the instructions were in French.

10-12. Without bothering to unplug the machine, Paula jumped in her car, drove to the computer store, and demanded that the manager give her a free tutorial!

Answer Key (cont.)

SUBORDINATION, page 49 (Answers may vary)

1-2. Although they boarded their windows against the storm, the windows were smashed. // The windows were smashed although they boarded them against the storm.

—The first sentence emphasizes the boarding of the windows, while the second stresses that the windows were smashed.

3-4. When the gopher left its hole unoccupied for the day, a snake slithered in and found a new home. // A snake slithered in and found a new home when the gopher left its hole unoccupied for the day.

—The second sentence highlights the snake finding a new home, while the first pays more attention to the fact that the gopher left its home unattended.

5-7. Since the cost of season tickets will increase an estimated 15%, fewer people will be able to attend games. // Fewer people will be able to attend games since the cost of season tickets will increase an estimated 15%.
—In the first sentence, the 15% increase is emphasized. "Fewer people..." is highlighted in the second.

8-10. I keep getting piles of useless junk mail every week despite the fact that I called the post office and complained. // Despite the fact that I called the post office and complained, I keep getting piles of useless junk mail.

—The fact that the person complained is emphasized more in the second sentence. The placement of the subordinate allows for an emphatic pause that the first sentence lacks.

11-12. When George went on the bike ride, he acted like Don Quixote. // George acted like Don Quixote when he went on the bike ride.

—The second version doesn't work: the pronoun "he" is ambiguous. It can refer to George or to Don Quixote!